LEARN TENNIS
IN A WEEKEND

LEARN TENNIS IN A WEEKEND

PAUL DOUGLAS

Photography by Matthew Ward

DORLING KINDERSLEY
London • New York • Stuttgart

A DORLING KINDERSLEY BOOK

Art Editor Kevin Ryan
Editor Jo Weeks
Series Editor James Harrison
Production Controller Meryl Silbert

First published in Great Britain in 1991
by Dorling Kindersley Limited,
9 Henrietta Street, London WC2E 8PS

A CIP catalogue record for this book is available from the British Library

ISBN 0-86318-594-0

Computer page make-up by The Cooling Brown Partnership
Reproduced by Colourscan, Singapore
Printed and bound in Italy by Arnoldo Mondadori, Verona.

CONTENTS

Introduction 6

PREPARING FOR THE WEEKEND 8

THE WEEKEND COURSE 26

Day 1

Day 2

AFTER THE WEEKEND 84

INTRODUCTION

WELCOME TO LEARN TENNIS IN A WEEKEND – a totally new concept in tennis learning. The basic fundamentals of playing tennis have altered little but the methods of presenting instruction, be they practical, on film or in book form, have developed into a modern art, based on proven ideas and new-found principles. My own approach to coaching tennis is founded upon simple instruction, teaching one thing at a time and giving clear and repetitive demonstrations of complete skills and strokeplay stages. I think that "having a go" yourself – before you settle down to learn from demonstrations and explanations – is a vital element in maintaining a natural feel for the game.

Visual learning has always been important – it now plays a major role in all sporting performance and tennis is no exception. *Learn Tennis in a Weekend* provides high quality pictures with pin-point instructions so that you can learn not only through physical on-court practice, but also by creating mind pictures of yourself mastering the skills and playing perfect strokes. Seeing yourself in continuous action accelerates the learning process, so put yourself in the on-the-move sequences that I have included as a back-up to the step-by-step build-up of strokeplay skills. *Learn Tennis in a Weekend* is an adventure and a challenge. I know that you will enjoy the adventure and I join you in the challenge. With the help of this book you will succeed. In closing my introduction I wish you good luck.

PAUL DOUGLAS

PREPARING FOR THE WEEKEND

Gain maximum benefit from your weekend by making advance preparations

BALLS
Buy a mixture of quality and second-grade balls (p.12).

FITNESS
Start getting fit before the weekend (pp.16–19).

CHOOSE A WEEKEND you can devote to your tennis without fear of interruption and arrange to have a tennis court at your disposal well in advance by hiring one from your local park or school. Ideally, plan to spend your weekend with a practice partner of similar ability who shares your enthusiasm for the game. If you are learning on your own you will need a practice wall or some form of ball-firing machine to act as your on-court partner.

It is important that you equip yourself properly. You may need two rackets because you won't want to be held up waiting for a restring halfway through the course. Get two or three cans of top quality balls for matchplay practice and 60 to 130 second-grade balls to fill up your ball-firing machine for strokeplay drills. For footwear, get purpose-

FOOTWEAR
Surface grip and comfort are paramount (p.13).

GRIPS
Different grips for different strokes (pp.20–21).

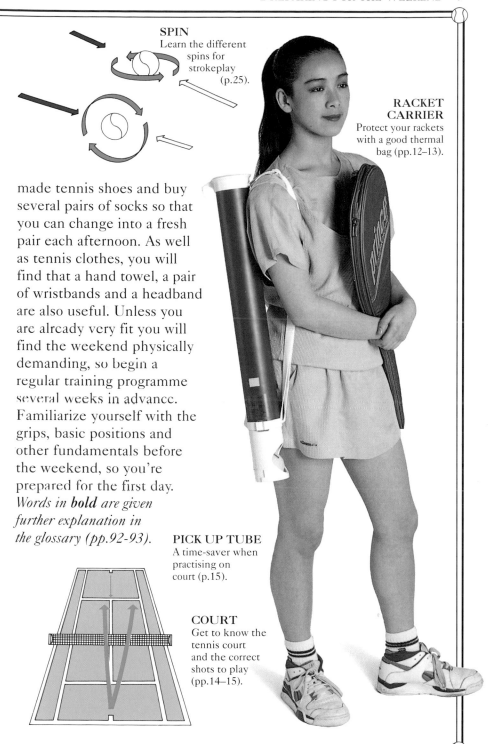

SPIN
Learn the different spins for strokeplay (p.25).

RACKET CARRIER
Protect your rackets with a good thermal bag (pp.12–13).

made tennis shoes and buy several pairs of socks so that you can change into a fresh pair each afternoon. As well as tennis clothes, you will find that a hand towel, a pair of wristbands and a headband are also useful. Unless you are already very fit you will find the weekend physically demanding, so begin a regular training programme several weeks in advance. Familiarize yourself with the grips, basic positions and other fundamentals before the weekend, so you're prepared for the first day. *Words in **bold** are given further explanation in the glossary (pp.92-93).*

PICK UP TUBE
A time-saver when practising on court (p.15).

COURT
Get to know the tennis court and the correct shots to play (pp.14–15).

TENNIS KIT

Choosing rackets, strings, balls, shoes and clothes

FOR YOUR WEEKEND you will need a decent racket, that suits your needs and abilities, and comfortable clothes, including a tracksuit if you have one. There are many different shapes and sizes of racket available. Most of these are variations on the slim-profiled "wide-body" type, which is the major advance in tennis racket design since wooden rackets went out of fashion. Wide-bodies are now accepted as the lightest and strongest frames in the world.

TOP CAP •
A plastic cup neatly embraces the shaft at the top of the handle.

THROAT •
The throat is usually open and its shape affects the degree of flex in the frame and the size of the **sweet spot**.

• SHOULDERS
The link between the frame head, the bridge and the shaft.

WIDE-BODIED RACKETS

The streamlined head and broad side-on dimensions of the wide-body racket means better manoeuvrability and stiffness. Wide-bodies are more powerful than the slimmer-bodied models and they can be more easily balanced to be light in the head.

• SHAFT
The shaft disperses vibration before shock waves from impact are passed on to the player via the handle.

• OVERGRIPS
Overgrips can be fitted to provide more "feel". Tightly wind the overgrip diagonally up the handle from the butt end. Secure it by overlapping the first wrap and taping it down at the end.

HANDLE
As the shaft enters the handle it may be covered by an octagonal foam rubber pallet. Frames are balanced with lead put into the pallet during production.

• BUTT END
The butt end is usually covered by a cap to provide support for the heel of your playing hand.

STRINGS

Strings range from thick 15 gauge to fine 17 gauge. There are two basic types of synthetic strings – monofilament and multifilament, which are generally superior.

BUMPER GUARD •
Protects the crown of the frame and the strings.

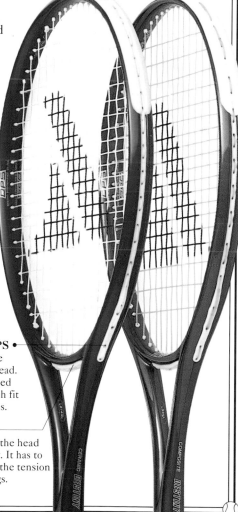

• *Main strings*

• *Cross strings*

• STRINGING PATTERN
The hitting surface must be flat. The strings are woven in a uniform pattern and are threaded through holes in the racket frame. String patterns are open or dense, i.e. large or small squares.

GROMMET STRIPS •
These wrap around the outside of the racket head. The strings are protected by the grommets, which fit through the string holes.

BRIDGE •
The bridge completes the head between the split shaft. It has to be strong to cope with the tension of at least 6 main strings.

CLOTHES

Wear comfortable clothes that are
easy to wash. Shorts and skirts should
not be too tight around the waistband
and shirts must allow your arms and
shoulders freedom to move. Wear
socks with cushioned soles and heels.

• HEADBANDS
Tie long hair back or use a headband
to keep your hair in place and stop
sweat running into your eyes.

TOWELLING WRISTLETS •
Absorbent towelling wristlets for
wiping your forehead and keeping
your palms dry.

RACKET CARRIERS •
Thermal racket bags protect up to 4 rackets
and the shoulder strap makes carrying easy.

TENNIS BALLS

TESTING TIME
Officially accepted tennis balls have to
undergo rigorous testing procedures
before they can be used in tournament
play. Always choose from leading
brands that are sold in pressurized
cans as it is bad for your game to play
with inferior tennis balls.

FOUR OR MORE
A can of 4 balls is enough for playing a
practice match but if you are working-
out using a ball machine
or doing exercises
with your partner
you will need a
hopper full of
tennis balls that
are at least
second grade.

**TENNIS
CLOTHES**
Clothes are
made of light,
washable fabrics.

EQUIPMENT CARRIERS •
Big pro-bags or tournament holdalls will
take every item of tennis equipment.

TENNIS BALLS •
A can of 4 tournament balls for
matchplay or as a serious practice set.

TENNIS SOCKS •
Good socks are cushioned to protect the balls
of the feet, the heels, and the achilles tendons.

TRACKSUITS
Warm-up outfits prepare you for action – keep them on for your pre-game stretching routine.

FOOTWEAR

SHOES
Protect your feet and improve your footwork by choosing good tennis shoes. They must provide flexibility and stability and give support to your instep, ankles, and achilles tendons. If you can only afford one pair of shoes, then cross-trainers are a good idea as they can be used for practically any sporting activity.

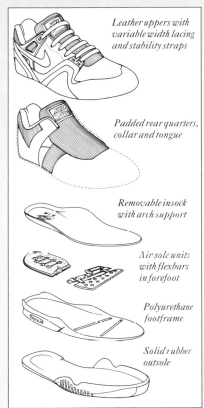

Leather uppers with variable width lacing and stability straps

Padded rear quarters, collar and tongue

Removable insock with arch support

Air sole units with flexbars in forefoot

Polyurethane footframe

Solid rubber outsole

SOLES
Select shoes to suit your game and the type of court you play on most often as different court surfaces require different soles: smooth soles for indoors, pimpled for grass, and herringbone for general use. These features are combined in this sole.

ON THE COURT

Know your court – the markings, the surfaces,
the net and extra equipment

THE RECTANGULAR TENNIS COURT that we know today was introduced for the very first Wimbledon Championships in 1877, when the current dimensions of 23.77 by 8.23m (78 by 27ft) for the singles court were agreed (see p.86 for full court measurements). Tennis was originally played on grass but it is now played on a variety of court surfaces, the majority of which are synthetic. The different surfaces produce different conditions of play, which can have a marked effect on your game.

COURT MARKINGS

Tennis lines are boundary lines and are named according to their function. For example, the baselines and sidelines limit the depth and width of your drives and volleys, while the service lines restrict the depth of your service.

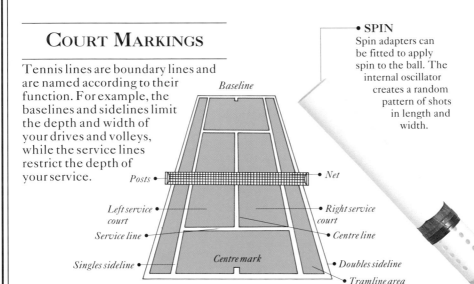

• SPIN
Spin adapters can be fitted to apply spin to the ball. The internal oscillator creates a random pattern of shots in length and width.

Baseline

Posts • — • *Net*

Left service court • — • *Right service court*

Service line • — • *Centre line*

Singles sideline • — *Centre mark* — • *Doubles sideline*

• *Tramline area*

COURT SURFACES

GRASS
Grass is a fast-playing surface but is difficult to maintain. Artificial grass is easy to maintain and can be fast or slow.

CLAY
Plays slow. Its top surface of fine or coarse sand requires regular maintenance.

CEMENT
Plays fast or slow depending on the texture of the top surface. When it is left rough the game will be markedly slower.

ASPHALT
Bitumen-based court needing little upkeep. Plays faster when sprayed with green paint.

THE NET

PROBLEM SOLVING

More than just a barrier strung across the court, the net dictates your strokeplay and the type of shot you play. It provides you with a problem for each shot and you have to find the best solution.

Posts 1.07m (3ft 6in) high and 0.91m (3ft) outside doubles sideline

Centre 0.91m (3ft) high

Singles sticks 0.91m (3ft) outside singles sideline

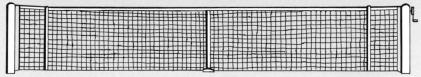

BALL MACHINES

Modern ball firing equipment is highly efficient. Even basic machines can be fitted with accessories that vary speed and depth, make the ball spin and simulate a complete matchplay rally.

PICK UP TUBE •

Retrievers/dispensers like this hold 18 balls and make practice play easy. The flared end picks up balls and the tube can be hung on a court fence.

PNEUMATIC BALL MACHINE

Powered by pneumatic propulsion, a ball machine such as this one holds 135 balls and will fire them every 3 seconds at speeds of up to 33m (110ft) per second. It measures 96.5cm (38in)x 56cm (22in)x 33cm (13in).

BALL RATE

Choice of 3-, 6-, or 12-second intervals.

WORK-OUTS

Weighing up to 14.5kg (32lb), ball machines are easy to manoeuvre on court.

TENNIS TRAINING

Exercise your muscles and limbs for general fitness to gain strength, stamina, speed, and flexibility on the court

STRENGTH, STAMINA, SPEED, AND FLEXIBILTY are the four major fitness factors for tennis, and each requires an exercise routine. 1. For strength and general fitness start off with the Super Six body-resistance exercises shown here. They are easy to do, so fitting them in to regular circuits should not be difficult. 2. For stamina, run several times a week. It's great for your heart and lungs. Try a few 800m ($^1/_2$ mile) jogs when preparing for the weekend. 3. For speed, do short, sharp sprints on the court from **sideline** to **sideline** and you'll soon be **running down** every ball when you rally. 4. For flexibility do a daily stretching routine.

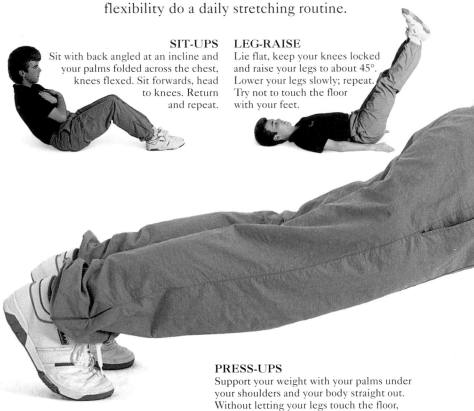

SIT-UPS
Sit with back angled at an incline and your palms folded across the chest, knees flexed. Sit forwards, head to knees. Return and repeat.

LEG-RAISE
Lie flat, keep your knees locked and raise your legs to about 45°. Lower your legs slowly; repeat. Try not to touch the floor with your feet.

PRESS-UPS
Support your weight with your palms under your shoulders and your body straight out. Without letting your legs touch the floor, breathe in and bend your arms. Now breathe out and straighten your arms again.

STEP-UPS
Step up with your left foot on to a bench about 50cm (20in) high, and then step down again with the same foot. Do an equal number of step-ups with your right foot. Keep your back straight and look forwards.

DOUBLE-KNEE JUMPS
Stand with your feet together. Crouch down and then leap in the air, bringing your knees up to your chest. Repeat non-stop.

SQUAT THRUST
Support your weight with your knees between your arms. Thrust backwards, straightening your body and legs and then come forwards again.

• FULLY ARMED
Doing press-ups is a great conditioner for your arms and shoulders. There's no need to lock-out your arms fully, or to dip too low.

CIRCUITS
Perform each exercise as many times as you can, resting 45 seconds between exercises. Half of each maximum you can do will be the right number for the first month. Go through your whole routine twice without resting. Note how long it takes you so that you can measure your progress. Set a new programme in the following month by completing maximums again and then halving them as before.

• FINGER FLEXING
If you're feeling really fit, try doing this one on your fingertips.

STRETCHING

Stretching is the best way to stay flexible for tennis. Spend between 10 and 20 seconds on each stretching exercise, taking it easy and enjoying the stretch. Go through your routine a second time, holding for a slightly longer and more progressive stretch. Spend 15 minutes stretching.

SEQUENCE
Try the stretches in this order: 7, 6, 4, 5, 1, 2, 3, 8. Remember to breathe normally. Do not hold your breath.

1 BODY TURN

Sit with your left leg straight and your right hand resting behind you. Bend your right knee and cross your right foot over your left leg, placing it by your left knee. Bend your left elbow and place it against the outside of your right leg above your knee. Turn your upper body and look over your right shoulder, resisting the turn with left elbow pressure.

2 TUMMY STRETCH

Lie flat on your stomach with your arms and legs straight out. Slide upright on your palms.

3 ARM/WRIST STRETCH

Support your weight as shown. Turn your hands so your thumbs are outside and your fingers point towards your knees.

4 MIDDLE AND LOWER LEG STRETCH

(Hamstring/calves/ achilles)
Stand about 30cm (1ft) from a wall and lean forwards on to it, resting your head on your crossed forearms. Bend your right knee and stretch your left leg backwards, keeping the left heel on the ground. Move your hips forwards.

5 UPPER LEG STRETCH

(Hips/hamstring/groin)
Take a large step forwards with your left leg, bending your knee and keeping it directly above your ankle. Keep your right leg extended backwards, heel off the floor. Lower your hips, applying pressure to forward movement of body weight.

6 KNEE STRETCH
(Front upper leg/quads)
Stand and place your right palm against a wall for support. Bend your left knee and grip the toe with your left hand, pulling your heel towards your buttock. Repeat with the other leg.

7 ARM CIRCLING
Swing your arms round together in slow, full circles. Repeat in opposite direction. Now clench your fists and repeat 5 circles each way.

PERFECT POSTURE •
Leg straight. Hips forwards. Knee bent and heel pulled in towards buttock.

SUPPORT •
Keep your right knee straight to support your body weight as you bend your left knee – and vice versa.

WARM-UP JOGGING
Always jog first to warm up your body. Jog around the tennis court 5 times and on your last 2 circuits add side-skips and running backwards.

8 HIP CIRCLING
Stand with your feet apart, hands on your hips, knees slightly flexed. Push your hips forwards and rotate. Circle in both directions.

GET TO GRIPS

How you hold the racket determines how you play the game

THE FEEL THAT YOU HAVE of the ball when it hits your
racket strings is communicated to you through your grip.
True grips – like the styles of play they encourage – are
either **Eastern, Western** or **Continental**. Here are seven
basic grips for both beginners and better players to select from. If
you are just starting, try the Eastern grips for **groundstroke** play
and your first sessions on the **volley**, and the Modified Eastern for
your first attempts at **serving**. Ultimately, you should graduate to
the Continental grip for all serve and volley play. The Modified
Continental grip, also known as the "Chopper" because you hold it
like a hatchet or small axe, is also ideal for **spin** serving.

GEARING UP TO THE BEST GRIP

SUPER SERVING
When you can serve most balls over the
net and get 50 per cent of them in, you are
ready to tackle the Modified **Continental**
– the best grip for all-round serving. It also
provides more freedom for wrist action.

QUICKFIRE VOLLEYS
As soon as you're happy up at the net, try
playing both **forehand** and **backhand**
volleys with the Modified **Continental**
grip. With no time to change your grip at
the net, sticking to one grip makes sense.

CONTINENTAL GRIP
Place the "V" between your
thumb and first finger to the
left of centre on the top
plane, with the knuckle of
your first finger on the upper
right slant or its bottom edge.

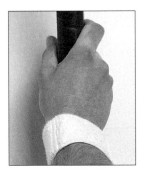

MODIFIED EASTERN FOREHAND GRIP
Place the "V" between your
thumb and first finger in the
centre of the top plane.
Wrap your thumb naturally
around the handle.

EASTERN BACKHAND GRIP
Place your "V" in the upper
left slant and your thumb
across the rear plane. The
knuckle of your first finger
is on the upper right slant.

EASTERN FOREHAND GRIP

"Shake hands" with your racket handle and you have the best forehand grip for beginners and top class players. With your palm behind the handle, this is a comfortable grip that gives you maximum strength for hitting any approaching ball.

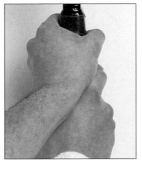

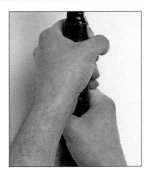

DOUBLE-HANDED 1

With the playing hand "V" between the **Continental** and the **Eastern Backhand** grip, place your support hand above it in an **Eastern Forehand** grip, with the heel nestling in the "V".

DOUBLE-HANDED 2

No need to change your grip after playing a forehand drive; just add your support hand above with a second **Eastern Forehand** grip. This makes racket support easy to begin with.

HAND-HELD

The racket is a natural extension of your hand – tennis evolved from *Jeu de Paume* (literally "game of the palm").

WRAPPING •
Wrap your thumb and fingers round the handle.

SEMI-WESTERN FOREHAND GRIP

Place your "V" on the upper right slant of the racket and the knuckle of your first finger on the top edge of the lower right slant; have your palm towards the bottom plane.

TRIGGER FINGER •

Spread your first finger slightly up the handle like a trigger finger, with its large knuckle on the rear plane.

"V" SHAPE •

Check that the "V" between your thumb and first finger is to the right of centre of the top plane.

WRIST •

Keep your wrist behind the handle and the heel of your hand at the butt end of the racket. Never choke your grip.

STANCE AND CONTROL

*Get to grips with the basic stances and hitting positions to help
you develop a good technique*

BASIC STANCES, HITTING POSITIONS and the various **spins** you can use
are fundamental to learning how to play tennis. The key to
improving the technique of your strokeplay is to begin from a sound
stance. Accurate judgment of the ball's flight plus early racket
preparation and footwork will bring you to the point of impact, with
your bodyweight perfectly balanced and your racket face correctly
angled, for the shot you are about to play. Your shot selection and
the type of spin you use for ball control are also fundamental to how
quickly your game will progress and how well you play.

READY POSITION

Face the net with your feet
shoulder-width apart, your
knees flexed, and your weight
over the balls of your feet. Hold
the racket centrally so you can
play any stroke with equal ease.

• EYES
Watch the player striking
the ball to pick up visual
clues about the nature of
your opponent's shot.

• RACKET
Support the racket
head by lightly
holding it at the
throat with your
non-playing hand.

• GRIP
Hold the racket
handle with a
forehand grip
(see p.20).

• FEET
Feet shoulder-
width apart for
stability. Knees
flexed to lower the
centre of gravity.

SIDE VIEW
When waiting to
volley, crouch down to
get your eyes in line
with any oncoming
shots from your
opponent. Keep your
elbows away from
your body to allow
freedom of movement.

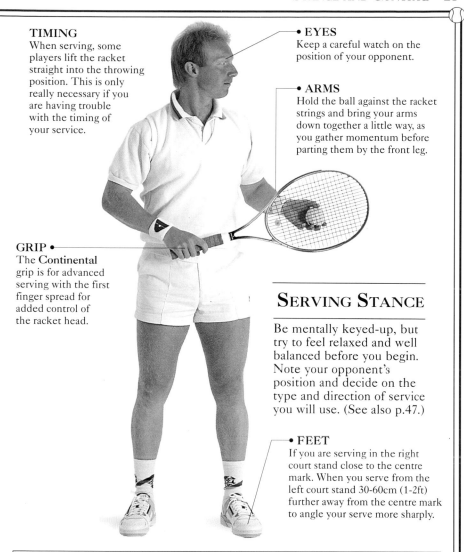

TIMING
When serving, some players lift the racket straight into the throwing position. This is only really necessary if you are having trouble with the timing of your service.

• EYES
Keep a careful watch on the position of your opponent.

• ARMS
Hold the ball against the racket strings and bring your arms down together a little way, as you gather momentum before parting them by the front leg.

GRIP •
The **Continental** grip is for advanced serving with the first finger spread for added control of the racket head.

SERVING STANCE

Be mentally keyed-up, but try to feel relaxed and well balanced before you begin. Note your opponent's position and decide on the type and direction of service you will use. (See also p.47.)

• FEET
If you are serving in the right court stand close to the centre mark. When you serve from the left court stand 30-60cm (1-2ft) further away from the centre mark to angle your serve more sharply.

THE FLIGHT OF THE BALL

THE TWO FLIGHTS
In **groundstroke** play the ball has two flights: the first as it leaves your opponent's racket and the second after the ball has bounced on your side of the net. When you begin to play tennis anticipating the second flight can be difficult. Try to judge where the ball will bounce and position yourself so that you are able to make a controlled return. Avoid rushing straight towards where it will bounce. The service also has two flights but the **volley** only one.

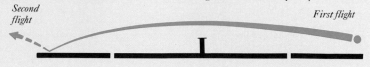

Second flight

First flight

CALLING THE SHOTS

DIFFERENT STROKES

A stroke is the action of hitting the ball, while a shot describes the flight and eventual destination of the ball after impact. Many tennis shots can be produced from different strokes, such as a **backhand** slice **approach shot** (see pp.80–81). Here are some shots to use in game situations.

APPROACH SHOT

An **approach shot** is any shot played prior to moving up court to **volley**. You can approach cross court or down-the-line or down-the-centre.

CROSS COURT AND DOWN-THE-LINE

Cross court shots are played diagonally, i.e. right court to right court. A **down-the-line** shot is hit parallel to the **sideline**.

DROP SHOT

A shot played to land just over the net with very little bounce is called a **drop shot**, and is usually played with underspin.

PASSING SHOT

A passing shot is when the ball is hit past your advacning opponent and may be hit **cross court** or **down-the-line**.

CHIP SHOT

A **chip** shot is a short blocked shot played with underspin and aimed to land at your opponent's feet or angled wide of him.

THE HIT

Try to be perfectly balanced, with your weight well down as you move forwards into a shot. In this example, the player keeps his wrist firm and his racket head above wrist level, as he plays a low **volley**.

• **ARM**
Left arm extended for balance.

• **FEET**
Feet well apart and stepping into the shot to create a low centre of gravity so adding stability to the shot.

USING SPIN

The amount and type of **spin** that you apply to the ball has a considerable affect on how the ball travels through the air and bounces. The spin itself will be affected by whether the ball bounces off the court or your racket strings.

SLICE SERVICE
The hit, right, shows the impact position of the slice service. The racket face has been angled to control the ball with **sidespin**.

RACKET FACE

The angle of your racket face has a direct bearing on the outcome of the shot.

OPEN FACE
An **open** racket face plays the ball upwards and encourages it to **spin** backwards.

CLOSED FACE
A **closed** racket face plays the ball down and encourages it to **spin** forwards.

FLAT FACE
A flat racket face plays the ball straight ahead before gravity pulls it downwards.

TYPES OF SPIN

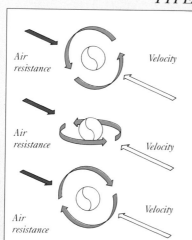

Air resistance   *Velocity*

Air resistance   *Velocity*

Air resistance   *Velocity*

TOPSPIN
The top of the ball spins forwards against air resistance, forcing the ball down. When you play topspin shots aim higher over the net than for a basic drive.

SIDESPIN
If the right hand side of the ball spins against air resistance, the ball swerves to the left and vice-versa. **Sidespin** is good for **serving** and **approach** play (see pp.80–81).

UNDERSPIN
The bottom of the ball spins against air resistance, which forces the ball upwards. Underspin shots need to travel much lower over the net than basic drives unless you are playing an underspin **lob** (see pp.74–5).

THE WEEKEND COURSE

Understanding the course at a glance

THE COURSE COVERS TWELVE skills, divided into two days of applied study and practice. The basic **groundstrokes**, **service** and service return are covered on the first day after you have developed a feel for ball and racket. The second day is devoted to the **volley**, **lob** and smash, and the matchplay skills of **approach play**, serve and volley. By the end of the first day you will be playing out points and by the end of the second day you will be ready for a game, set or even a practice match. Different people progress at different speeds, so don't give up just because you are behind the clock.

Basic serve

DAY 1		Hours	Page
SKILL 1	Basic Ball Sense	1	28-31
SKILL 2	Forehand Drive	1-1^1/$_2$	32-37
SKILL 3	Backhand Drive	1-1^1/$_2$	38-43
SKILL 4	Double-handed Backhand	1^1/$_2$	44-45
SKILL 5	Service	1	46-55
SKILL 6	Service Return	1	56-59

Follow through

Grip switch

KEY TO SYMBOLS

CLOCKS
Clocks appear on the first page of each new skill. They highlight, through the blue coloured section, how long you might spend and show where a particular skill fits in your day. For example, check the clock on p.32. The grey segment shows that 1 hour has been spent on the previous skill, and that now 1½ hours is advised for Skill 2: Setting Up, as shown by the blue section.

RATING SYSTEM
Each skill is given a points rating according to its degree of difficulty. One bullet (•) denotes that the skill is comparatively straightforward, while 5 bullets (•••••) are given to the most challenging skills.

MICRO-MEN
The series of micro-men, alongside each skill, highlight number of steps involved. Blue-coloured players identify the photographic step.

Visualization

Smash

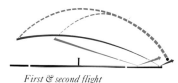

First & second flight

DAY 2		Hours	Page
SKILL 7	Forehand Volley	1	60-63
SKILL 8	Backhand Volley	1	66-71
SKILL 9	Lob Defence	1	72-75
SKILL 10	Smash Attack	1	76-79
SKILL 11	Approach Play	1	80-81
SKILL 12	Serve & Volley	1	82-83

Slice & spin

Volley practice tip

Volley

SKILL

1

BASIC BALL SENSE

Definition: *Developing your natural reactions to a moving ball in order to perform simple skills*

THROW A TENNIS BALL back and forth with a partner to test your reactions and judge your ball sense. Begin your session with easy throwing and catching exercises on your own, and then play throw/catch with a partner. Progress from fairly static exercises to on the move practices. Set each other challenges – like "first to do 10 in a row" – to inspire greater efforts and improve concentration.

OBJECTIVE: To develop and apply ball sense when driving, **serving** and **volleying**.
Rating • to ••••• according to your natural ability.

BOUNCE AND CATCH

Throw a ball back and forth with a partner and catch it before the bounce. Now bounce the ball off the court midway between you, catching it as it falls towards the second bounce between knee and waist height.

DEVELOPING ABILITY
Stretch your abilities by throwing a ball to each other simultaneously, as the players are doing here. Start by throwing the ball straight across to each other, catching on the **volley**, then try bouncing the balls down to each other. When this becomes easy, try throwing straight across while your partner bounces his ball down, and change the pattern every few seconds by calling "switch".

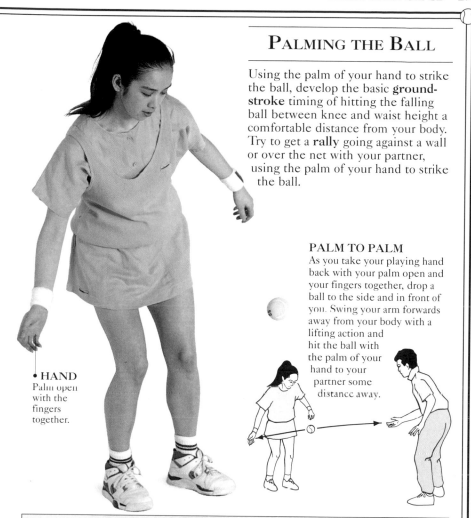

PALMING THE BALL

Using the palm of your hand to strike the ball, develop the basic **ground-stroke** timing of hitting the falling ball between knee and waist height a comfortable distance from your body. Try to get a **rally** going against a wall or over the net with your partner, using the palm of your hand to strike the ball.

• HAND
Palm open with the fingers together.

PALM TO PALM
As you take your playing hand back with your palm open and your fingers together, drop a ball to the side and in front of you. Swing your arm forwards away from your body with a lifting action and hit the ball with the palm of your hand to your partner some distance away.

SHORT TENNIS

DEVELOPING BASIC SKILLS
Short or mini tennis is ideal for developing your ball sense skills and is a good game in itself. It is played on a badminton-sized court – 13.4 x 6.1m (44 x 20ft) – with the centre-net height at 80cm (2 ft 7in). Rackets are short, lightweight and mainly plastic, and the ball is soft foam or low compression.

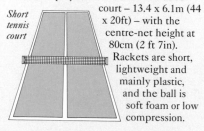

Short tennis court

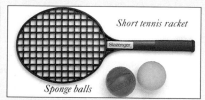

Short tennis racket

Slazenger

Sponge balls

Scoring is on "first to 11 points" basis, with a 2-point lead required after 10–10. As a cheaper version of tennis, it's popular for teaching children how to graduate to the full size game, but adults can also develop hand-eye co-ordination skills from it.

CATCH CONTROL

HAND–EYE CO-ORDINATION

Ball sense exercises are vital for improving hand and eye co-ordination. Try to get into the habit of doing these exercises whenever you have some free time.

1 Chuck a ball in the air and catch it as it falls. Catch with both hands and then with your playing hand only.

2 Throw a ball up with your left hand and catch it with your right and vice versa.

3 Bounce the ball off the court and catch it as it falls, at first with both hands, and then try with one hand.

4 Bounce the ball higher off the court and turn a full circle before catching it.

A FLEXIBLE APPROACH

Try playing other games to improve your ball sense. Basketball is a good conditioner, and will add flexibility to your movements.

ACT–REACT

With your partner facing away from you, call his name and then throw a tennis ball towards him. He must turn quickly, react to the ball and catch it. Now it's your turn. You must not turn until your name is called.

EYE CONTACT •
Listen for your name, turn quickly and look for the ball.

HANDS •
Seek out the ball with both eye and hand contact.

HIPS •
Improve your sense of balance by twisting from the hips rather than turning around.

MORE SKILLS
When the basic act-react exercise becomes easy, delay calling until after the ball is on its way. Develop it even further by waiting until the ball has almost reached your partner before calling.

BALL CONTROL

To get you used to altering your angle of racket face as well as to strengthen your wrist, try bouncing the ball up off the strings, then flip the racket head over so that the next bounce comes off the other surface of your strings. Keep flipping the racket face between hits.

• HOLD AND GRIP
Use a natural grip and hold the racket out before bouncing the ball up off your strings.

BEAM BOUNCE
Bouncing the ball off the racket head's edge or beam is the hardest bounce exercise to master. Keep your grip very steady and just make slight upward movements of the racket head to gain complete control of the ball.

• STANCE
Stand with your feet shoulder-width apart and your knees slightly flexed.

SWINGING, THROWING, AND PUNCHING

STREAMERS
Attach paper or cloth streamers to your racket to practise the 3 basic actions in tennis – swinging, throwing and punching. The streamers show you that racket head speed is needed for throwing and swinging while punching requires hardly any. Swinging is used in **groundstroke** play where pace has to be generated to return the ball swiftly. Throwing is needed for serving, when maximum racket head speed is needed to impart pace to an almost still ball, and for overhead smashing. In volleying, punching is used to redirect the power of the ball towards its new target.

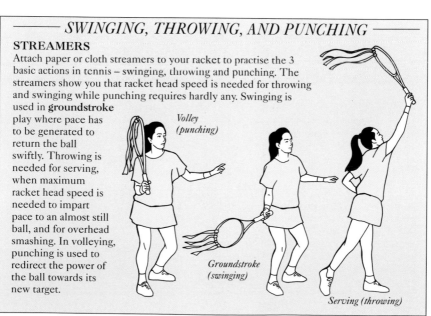

Volley (punching)

Groundstroke (swinging)

Serving (throwing)

SKILL

2

FOREHAND DRIVE

Definition: *The most natural* **groundstroke** *which can be played from both a closed and a semi-open stance*

THE FOREHAND DRIVE is the major groundstroke for both the beginner and the advanced player. Like warriors of old carrying swords in their right hands and shields in their left, tennis players have a natural urge to attack the ball on the **forehand** side. If you feel this natural urge, go for it and develop an aggressive approach from the beginning. Remember: a tennis player without an attacking **forehand** drive is like a gunfighter without a gun.

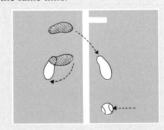

OBJECTIVE: An all round attacking stroke that dictates play from the **back court** and sets up net play chances. *Rating* ••

AIMING, TIMING AND CONTROL

Arcing flight guarantees good margin for error.

SHAPE OF SHOT
To hit your **forehand** and backhand drives deep to the far **baseline**, aim another net's height, or roughly 1m (3ft), over the net.

FORMING A LOOP
Relax your elbow at the end of the **take back** and let your racket head form a natural **loop** to add rhythm and speed.

SHOULDER AIM
At the preparation, turn your shoulders until your non-hitting shoulder is aiming at the oncoming ball. This helps you to line-up the ball and improve your timing and control through the **hitting zone**.

FOOTWORK
Position yourself sideways-on to the ball by simply turning on your right foot and stepping in with your left. Practise your footwork and shadow your **groundstroke** at the same time.

COURT PRACTICE

CROSS COURT

Drop balls for each other to hit over the net and then progress to throwing balls underarm to simulate an opponent's shot. If this goes well, graduate to hitting some **cross court** drives to each other, from **baseline** to baseline. When you can do a 10-shot **rally**, have a go at 20, always trying to hit deep into each other's forehand corners. Move back behind your **centre marks** between shots to keep on the move. Beginners should start from mid-court, moving back as their skill improves.

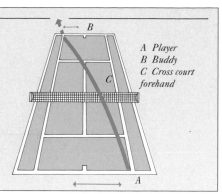

A *Player*
B *Buddy*
C *Cross court forehand*

• BALANCE
As you turn away release your non-playing hand for balance. To provide a postive feeling of lift in the forward swing let your racket head form a natural loop.

—————— Step 2 ——————

TAKE BACK

Turn **sideways-on** from the **ready position**, release your **non-playing hand** and flex your knees as you take the racket back early at the hitting height. At the end of your take back start to form a loop with your racket head.

• GRIP
Use the **"Shake hands"** grip and remember to spread your index finger up the handle for extra racket head control.

• KNEES
Turn on your right foot and let your knees bend.

• LEFT FOOT
Be ready to step in as your forward swing begins.

SKILL
2

———— Step 3 ————
THE HIT

Step in with your left foot
and swing the racket
head up to meet the
ball as it falls
between knee
and waist
height.

**RACKET
ARM'S
DISTANCE**
Really extend
your racket arm
at the hit. If you
hit with your elbow bent you are too
close to the ball and may lose power
and control over your shot.

HEAD •
Keep your head steady
and eyes on the ball.

• **SHOULDER**
Swing your right
shoulder powerfully
into the hit.

**SWING
ACTION** •
Swing the racket
head from hip to
hip to achieve
perfect stroke play.

• **FIRMNESS**
Squeeze your grip
and keep your wrist
firm at impact.

• **KNEE**
Transfer your weight
forwards over your
bending left knee to
create a sound
hitting platform.

• **FEET**
Keep your feet
parallel and
more than
shoulder-width
apart to keep
stable as you
make the hit.

TACTICAL USES
Play deep drives **cross
court** to your opponent's
forehand corner or **down-
the-line** to his backhand
corner or go for an angled
cross court drive (one
that bounces near the
service line and **sideline**).

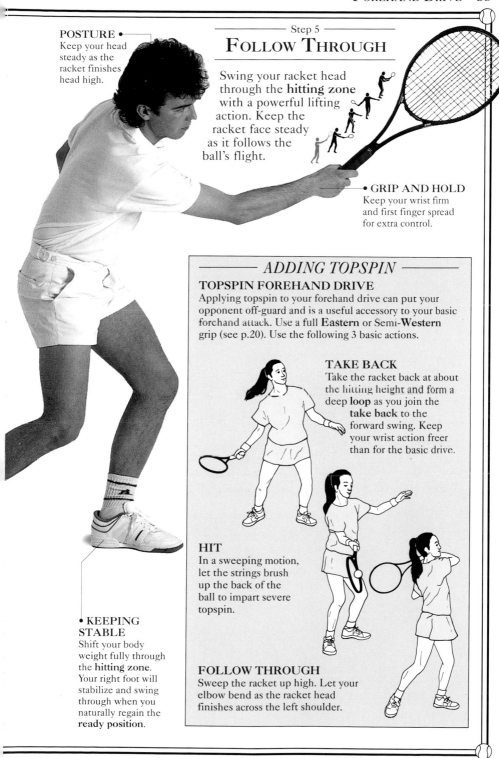

POSTURE
Keep your head steady as the racket finishes head high.

Step 5
FOLLOW THROUGH

Swing your racket head through the **hitting zone** with a powerful lifting action. Keep the racket face steady as it follows the ball's flight.

GRIP AND HOLD
Keep your wrist firm and first finger spread for extra control.

ADDING TOPSPIN

TOPSPIN FOREHAND DRIVE
Applying topspin to your forehand drive can put your opponent off-guard and is a useful accessory to your basic forehand attack. Use a full **Eastern** or Semi-**Western** grip (see p.20). Use the following 3 basic actions.

TAKE BACK
Take the racket back at about the hitting height and form a deep **loop** as you join the **take back** to the forward swing. Keep your wrist action freer than for the basic drive.

HIT
In a sweeping motion, let the strings brush up the back of the ball to impart severe topspin.

FOLLOW THROUGH
Sweep the racket up high. Let your elbow bend as the racket head finishes across the left shoulder.

KEEPING STABLE
Shift your body weight fully through the **hitting zone**. Your right foot will stabilize and swing through when you naturally regain the **ready position**.

FOREHAND DRIVE IN ACTION

Static work is good practice, but when it comes to competing generally, a more dynamic approach is required. This on-the-move sequence shows you how to prepare your racket and position your feet as you approach the **hitting area**. The hitting platform is solid, yet the movement flows from start to finish, allowing you to run on for your next shot or recover to your previous base.

ATTACKING PLAY

PLACEMENT
Play **forehand** drives deep to your opponent's forehand and **backhand** corners to pin him in the **backcourt**. Aim your shots **cross court** and wait for him to switch to a **down-the-line** drive, then it will be easier to return the ball.

• TAKE BACK
Begin your take back before you reach the **hitting area** or you will have to prepare and make your shot all in one.

• FOOTWORK
Turn **sideways-on** and set off with either foot, adjusting your footwork as you go.

ANGLED DRIVE

TACTICS

A useful ploy is to hit angled **cross court** drives, as shown here. The shot landing near the **sideline** and between the **service line** and **baseline** takes your opponent out wide for his return, opening up the court for your next shot.

• MOMENTUM
On wide balls let your back foot swing through after impact, using it to launch you off towards your next location.

FOLLOW THROUGH •
Finish with your basic follow through, but if you are in **no man's land** you may have to lower your **trajectory** and stay down to keep your shot in court.

UNWIND •
Sound positioning parallel to the ball's flight will result in a natural unwinding movement as you step into the ball.

SKILL

3

BACKHAND DRIVE

Definition : *Groundstroke partner of the forehand drive*

THE BACKHAND STROKE has a much neater and less energy-sapping **take back** than the **forehand**. A sound grip and full body turn will enable you to uncoil into the hit like a striking rattlesnake. Use the full **Eastern backhand** grip.

OBJECTIVE: Initially to offer sound defence. Then to develop as a counter-attacking weapon. *Rating* •• with grip change.

Step 2

INITIAL TAKE BACK

From the **ready position**, face the net from behind your **baseline**. Hold the racket in front, supporting it at the throat with your non-playing hand, and ready for an instant grip change.

• **HEAD**
Keep your head steady as you begin turning to your left in the early **take back.**

• **GRIP**
Start with the "**Shake hands**" (**Eastern**) **forehand** grip, changing your grip by feel.

KNEES •
Keep your knees relaxed, bending your back knee more as you turn away.

FEET •
Balancing forwards, turn on your left foot, letting your weight move on to it as you take back the racket.

THE GRIP SWITCH
Steady the racket and turn your playing hand inwards around the handle till the "V" between thumb and forefinger lines up with the racket's inner edge.

Step 3

FULL TAKE BACK

Turn your shoulders more and shift your weight on to your left foot. Keep your support hand at the racket throat as you bring it behind your left hip.

STANCE •
Look over your hitting shoulder at the on-coming ball.

HIP •
Pivot your whole body around, and try to get your hips parallel to the flight of the ball, as you take the racket back at about hitting height.

POISED TO HIT
Complete the **take back** with your back facing towards the net. Your spare hand still supports the racket and your weight is poised, ready to be transferred forwards as your body uncoils and your right foot steps in.

• GET DOWN
Let your back knee bend as you turn away and really get down to play your shot.

BACKHAND HINTS

AWKWARD APPROACH
If the ball is coming at you, step away from its flight with your front foot. As you transfer your weight on to this foot, lean away from the ball so that you can extend your racket arm fully at the hit. Stay with the ball in the follow through as you return the ball along its original flight path.

PRACTISE FOR POWER
If you find it hard to get your shoulders far enough around to put any real power into your hit, try standing with your back facing the net. Get your partner to drop the ball to your side and behind you at racket arm's distance. Watch the ball over your shoulder as you turn and step in to do the **backhand**.

FOOTWORK
From the ready position, turn on your left foot and step in parallel to the ball's flight with your right foot as you hit. The key to sound footwork is accurate placing of your rear foot as you reach the **hitting zone**.

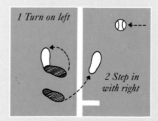

1 Turn on left

2 Step in with right

SKILL

3

Step 4

THE HIT

Release your support hand, and make a shallow **loop** with the racket head to ensure a low to high forward swing as you step in.

RACKET ANGLE •
Maintain your racket face angle in the high follow through.

BIRD'S EYE VIEW
From above, note how the hit occurs out in front but racket arm's distance away in the **sideways-on** position. Your backhand grip will give you a feeling of solidity at impact and provide a natural racket face angle for lift and direction.

HAND ACTION •
The **Eastern backhand** grip and a firm wrist will develop a powerful and well controlled backhand drive.

CONCENTRATE •
Watch the ball and track it to the hitting point with your eyes. Keep your head still.

• BALANCE
After releasing your support hand from the racket, extend it for balance.

• ANGLED HIT
Hold your racket arm straight at impact with your wrist locked. Your racket face should be angled back slightly to encourage lift.

• WEIGHT
Transfer your body weight on to your bent front knee as you sweep the racket head upwards to meet the ball. Keep your back toe on court.

FEET •
Step your front foot in parallel to the ball's line of flight to ensure a solid hitting platform.

THE CRITICAL SWING

ROOM

Give yourself plenty of room to swing out and up to meet the ball. Begin the step in and forward swing together. Joining the back and forward swing with a shallow **loop**, swing your racket from low to high through the **hitting zone**.

POWER

The easy power in the **backhand** comes from the uncoiling or unwinding action of your body and playing arm. To deliver power with control pivot on your back foot

and turn your hitting shoulder until your back faces the net. With your racket prepared behind your rear hip you are ready to uncoil with power and accuracy.

FRISBEE

You can develop "uncoil" power by throwing a frisbee back and forth to your partner. Then try sending a racket-head cover skimming over the net from one **baseline** to the other with the same **backhand** movement.

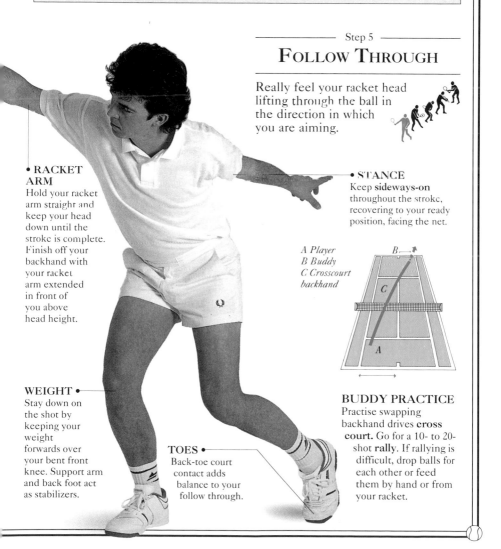

Step 5

FOLLOW THROUGH

Really feel your racket head lifting through the ball in the direction in which you are aiming.

• RACKET ARM

Hold your racket arm straight and keep your head down until the stroke is complete. Finish off your backhand with your racket arm extended in front of you above head height.

• STANCE

Keep **sideways-on** throughout the stroke, recovering to your ready position, facing the net.

A Player
B Buddy
C Crosscourt
backhand

WEIGHT •

Stay down on the shot by keeping your weight forwards over your bent front knee. Support arm and back foot act as stabilizers.

TOES •

Back-toe court contact adds balance to your follow through.

BUDDY PRACTICE

Practise swapping backhand drives **cross court**. Go for a 10- to 20- shot **rally**. If rallying is difficult, drop balls for each other or feed them by hand or from your racket.

BACKHAND DRIVE IN ACTION

The ability to combine your turn and run with your stroke preparation and positioning in the **hitting area** can be developed through regular practice. This sequence illustrates how the player's fluidity of movement saves time and energy – producing apparently effortless shot-making. With the on-the-move **backhand** drive added to your **groundstroke** repertoire you will now be master of the **back court**.

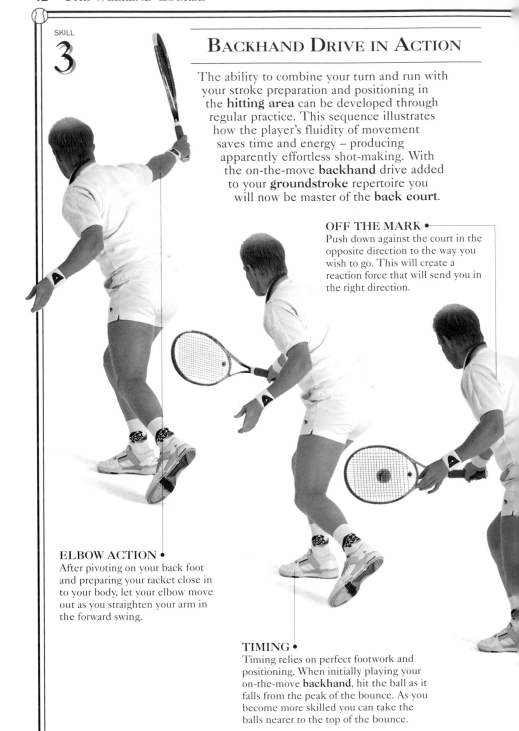

OFF THE MARK
Push down against the court in the opposite direction to the way you wish to go. This will create a reaction force that will send you in the right direction.

ELBOW ACTION
After pivoting on your back foot and preparing your racket close in to your body, let your elbow move out as you straighten your arm in the forward swing.

TIMING
Timing relies on perfect footwork and positioning. When initially playing your on-the-move **backhand**, hit the ball as it falls from the peak of the bounce. As you become more skilled you can take the balls nearer to the top of the bounce.

BALL VARIATIONS

THE CLOSE BALL

If a ball is coming at you, step away from its flight path with your front foot. As you transfer your body weight onto this foot, lean away from the ball so that you can fully extend your racket arm at the hit. Then stay with the ball in the follow through as you return the ball along its original flightpath.

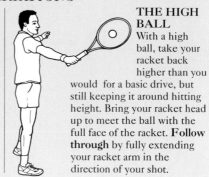

THE HIGH BALL

With a high ball, take your racket back higher than you would for a basic drive, but still keeping it around hitting height. Bring your racket head up to meet the ball with the full face of the racket. **Follow through** by fully extending your racket arm in the direction of your shot.

• BUILD-UP

Approach the ball on a curving run to get behind and parallel to its line of flight. Start your take back early, using a simple sidestep to reach the hitting area.

4 DOUBLE-HANDED BACKHAND

Definition : *An optional groundstroke partner for the forehand drive*

THE **DOUBLE-HANDED BACKHAND** is a perfect option for young players who lack physical strength and for older players just starting out. The two-handed stroke will encourage you to attack the ball with topspin and provides a feeling of greater strength and control.

OBJECTIVE: A counter-attacking stroke. *GRIPS :* Grip 1 (change) Grip 2 (add hand). *Rating* •• with grip 1 • with grip 2

—— Step 1 ——
TAKE BACK

As you pivot, add your other hand and take your racket back below your intended hitting height.

—— Step 2 ——
THE HIT

Step in with your right foot, swinging your racket to meet the ball in front of your leading hip.

GRIP •
Powerful two-handed grip provides you with strength and control.

HEAD DOWN •
The racket head points downwards.

MOTION •
Let your racket sweep out and up through the ball.

• WEIGHT
Weight has shifted forwards on to front leg.

• BALANCE
Weight gathered over flexed knee of back leg.

GRIP CHANGE

TECHNIQUE
Support your racket with your spare hand and turn your playing hand inwards until the "V" shape between thumb and first finger is on the inner edge of the handle (see also Grips p.21). Slide your support hand down to form a left-handed **forehand** grip above the right hand.

Ready position   *Backhand change*

HEIGHT •
Finish high for topspin effect.

— Step 3 —
FOLLOW THROUGH

Allow your body to uncoil fully as you drive through the ball. Rotation of the upper body and a high finish will add extra topspin for increased control, but you must stay down on the shot to maintain pace.

WRIST ACTION •
A firm-wristed swing with arms extended in the direction of your shot places emphasis on pace rather than **spin**. Whipping the racket head with a pronounced wrist action will impart more topspin to the ball.

PACE
For more pace with slightly less **spin**, follow through more in the direction of shot, as with the basic **backhand** drive (see p.41).

TOPSPIN •
High elbows produce brushed topspin for greater control.

KNEE •
Transfer your weight fully onto your bent front knee.

• STABILITY
Back foot stabilizes finish.

SKILL 5

THE SERVICE

DAY 1

Definition: *The crucial stroke of the game because it begins and can end every point*

THE SERVICE IS THE MOST DEVASTATING stroke in tennis. From a motionless – and seemingly harmless – beginning, the well-timed service will fire tennis balls into your opponent's court at cannonball speed. From your ankles upwards, you should feel a gathering of momentum rising rhythmically through your body, as your legs, hips, stomach, back, shoulders, playing arm and wrist create a chain reaction of power that results in an "anatomic" explosion at impact. Go for a modified **Eastern forehand** grip to begin with, graduating to the **Continental** grip.

OBJECTIVE: To dictate the run of play and set up winning situations. *Rating* ••• to ••••• depending on natural ability.

THROWING ACTION

The service action is simply an overarm throw. If you can throw a ball, you can serve.

1 From behind the **baseline** take turns with your partner at throwing a ball over the net towards the baseline on the far side of the court.

2 Make it bounce near the line or even hit the fence before it bounces.

3 After about 5 throws each, throw your next batch of balls into one of the diagonally opposite service courts.

4 Still taking turns, throw 5 to the right and then 5 to the left **service courts**. If you still can't send the ball far enough, turn your shoulders a bit more to increase your distance.

HOLDING THE BALL

GRASPING ACTION
To hold a ball, grasp it with your non-playing hand between your thumb and all four fingers. To hold 2 tennis balls grip the first ball with your thumb and first 2 fingers and hold the second ball against your hand with your third and fourth fingers. Then hold the ball or balls against the racket strings.

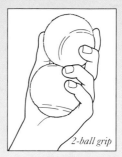

1-ball grip

2-ball grip

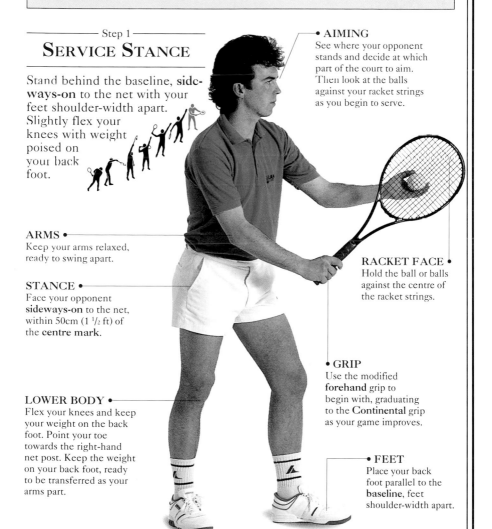

——— Step 1 ———
SERVICE STANCE

Stand behind the baseline, **sideways-on** to the net with your feet shoulder-width apart. Slightly flex your knees with weight poised on your back foot.

• **AIMING**
See where your opponent stands and decide at which part of the court to aim. Then look at the balls against your racket strings as you begin to serve.

ARMS •
Keep your arms relaxed, ready to swing apart.

STANCE •
Face your opponent **sideways-on** to the net, within 50cm (1 ½ ft) of the **centre mark**.

RACKET FACE •
Hold the ball or balls against the centre of the racket strings.

LOWER BODY •
Flex your knees and keep your weight on the back foot. Point your toe towards the right-hand net post. Keep the weight on your back foot, ready to be transferred as your arms part.

• **GRIP**
Use the modified **forehand** grip to begin with, graduating to the **Continental** grip as your game improves.

• **FEET**
Place your back foot parallel to the **baseline**, feet shoulder-width apart.

SKILL

5

EYES •
Look up along your left
arm at the ball.

• RACKET
Point the hitting face of
your racket head down-
wards and create a
diagonal line from
racket tip
to ball.

• ARMS
Fully extend
your throwing
arm before you
release the ball,
letting your shoulders
turn slightly, and
keeping the elbow of
your serving arm flexed
as you take back the
racket behind you.

--------- Step 2 ---------
SERVICE TAKE BACK

Slowly swing your arms down,
parting them at the hip. Let
the racket swing past
your body and
transfer your
weight over
your
flexed
knee.

• HIP
As your weight is
transferred on to the
front knee push your hip
forwards to establish a
sound hitting platform.

• FRONT FOOT
Keep your front foot
anchored to act as a
launch pad.

BACK FOOT •
Keep your back foot in
contact with the ground
to stabilize weight
transference.

--------- *PRACTISING SERVICE SKILLS* ---------

PLACING THE BALL
1 Take up the **service** stance, holding 1
ball against the strings. Move both arms
down a little way together for rhythm.

2 Part them, letting your racket swing
back while you stretch up with your left
arm to place the ball up to about twice the
height of your outstretched arm.

3 Keep your hand up and catch the ball as
it drops. Practise over and over again until
the ball falls directly into your hand
without your having to move it.

POSITIONING YOUR FEET
Stand a ball's width behind the **baseline** and
within 50cm (1½ ft) of the **centre mark**. For
feet placing, visualize a line drawn across the
front of your toes aiming to your target area.

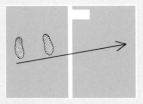

AVOIDING MISTAKES

FOOT FAULTS

The most common **foot fault** is treading on the **baseline** with the front foot before striking the ball. Chief culprits are transferring weight too late or standing with feet too close together in the serving stance (see pp.23, 47).

• PLACE-UP PEAK
Point the racket head and placing hand up as the ball reaches its peak.

Step 3

PLACE-UP

Place the ball up in front of you and a little to your right. As you release the ball, bend your racket arm and lift your racket until the tip points skywards. At the completion of the **place-up**, both your arms should point upwards.

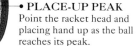

GRIP •
Serve with the Modified Forehand grip initially, but adopt the **Continental** grip as soon as you can, because it provides much greater scope for developing the necessary serving skills of wrist snap and racket arm extension.

RACKET ARM •
Keep the racket arm away from your body and its elbow high as you prepare to drop the racket head into the throwing position.

• FLEXED KNEE
Your front knee should be flexed to take your weight as you move forwards.

ANCHORING •
Keep the back foot firmly in contact with the court.

SKILL

5

RELEASING THE BALL •
Your outstretched **place-up** arm will drop away when you throw your racket head up to meet the ball.

• SHOULDER
By keeping the left shoulder high you will create a rising line through the shoulders for maximum thrust.

——— Step 4 ———

THROWING POSITION

Don't stop, but feel a pause at the height of the take-up, then let your racket head drop downwards smoothly into the throwing position deep between your shoulder blades.

PISTON POWER
Think of this position as a cylinder and your racket as a piston. The descending racket gathers velocity and accelerates as it comes up, gaining maximum speed just before the hit.

ELBOW •
Keeping the racket clear of your body, relax your elbow and let the racket head drop into the throwing position.

WALL WORK

THE PRACTICE WALL
Use the practice wall to improve your basic strokes. When practising a serve, stand behind a line 5-6m (15-20ft) from the wall. First hit a few serves down, then work on different aspects one at a time – like **place-up** and weight shift – before putting them back into the whole stroke to measure your progress.

• KNEE
Maintain the balance over your bent front knee prior to the racket launch.

ANCHORING •
The trailing leg stabilizes your throwing position as momentum gathers.

Step 5

THE HIT

Straighten your legs and launch the racket head up. Your body will be fully stretched out at impact, with just the toes in contact with the ground.

• RACKET
Hit the back of the ball with the middle of the strings.

STRAIGHT ARMS
You should be striking the ball at full racket-arm's reach in line with your hitting shoulder. Practise placing the ball a little to your right so that your racket arm is fully extended straight up from your shoulder. At the hit, the **place-up** arm drops away to help balance the body.

STRETCH •
Develop a catapult effect by fully stretching your right side.

• SHOULDER
Turn your hitting shoulder in powerfully as you throw your racket head up to meet the ball.

— IMPROVING CONTROL —

TOPSPIN MARGIN
Even the flattest of serves should carry some topspin for control, so try to develop the feeling that you are hitting up, through and over the ball. This will improve both your accuracy and your margin for error over the net. A ball served with a slight arcing flight also enlarges the target area.

• LEGS
Straighten your legs at the hit, with your back foot no longer anchored and ready for follow through action.

SKILL
5

• RACKET SWING

Let your racket swing past your left side as your left hand swings back to aid your balance.

RECOVERY

As your weight comes down, let your right knee bend to assist your recovery back behind the **baseline** to **rally**, or to act as a first powerful step of your forward run if you are moving in to **volley**.

• EYES

Keep your eye on the ball as you follow through.

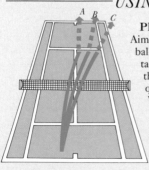

—— Step 7 ——

FOLLOW THROUGH

After impact allow your racket to swing down past your left leg in a full follow through, while letting your right foot swing across the **baseline** to restore your balance.

• WEIGHT

Finish the basic serve with your weight firmly on your right foot.

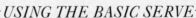

USING THE BASIC SERVE

PERCENTAGE SERVES

Aim to get 70 per cent of your first balls into court and maintain the tactical advantage. To achieve this, practise serving at three quarter's speed, not flat out. When you can serve either wide, straight at the body or down the centre, against right or left-handed players with consistency, you will be good enough to win most of your service games.

Left service court,
right-handed receiver
A Forehand, B Body, C Backhand

Right service court,
right-handed receiver
A Forehand, B Body, C Backhand

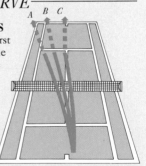

SLICE SERVICE

• RACKET FACE
The racket strings should cut around the right side of the ball at 3 o'clock.

• GRIP
Use the flexible, wrist-snapping **Continental** grip.

• FOCUS
Keep your head steady and your eyes focused firmly on the ball.

RACKET ARM •
Keep straight at impact.

RECOVERY •
Your stabilizing back foot will swing forwards to recovery when your racket follows through down past your left leg as in the basic serve.

• SHOULDERS
Allow your shoulders to turn in at the hit.

SECOND SERVICE
The slice **service** is the cutting edge of your service firepower. The slice delivery swerves sharply through the air before and after the bounce, staying low as it takes your opponent out of court. **Sidespin** makes it safe, so it is ideal to use as your second serve.

Flat serve   *Slice serve*

RACKET-FACE ANGLE
Turn your shoulders more for the slice than the flat serve. After the shoulders have turned in, the racket face is angled at impact (above right), while the full face of the racket meets the ball in the basic serve (above left). Practise brushing your racket strings up, across and around the outside of the ball.

FEET POSITIONS
Stand more **sideways-on** for the slice serve by moving your rear foot back slightly. Place the ball up in front of you and a little to your right.

SKILL

5

THE SERVICE IN ACTION

Although it is delivered from a specific on-court position, the **service** is not a static stroke. It may be on the spot, but from conception to completion the service should flow smoothly through many stages of on-the-move action. Here the service has been strung out to create a picture of the continuous movement that is vital to the serve. Imagine you are the server and place the stages one on top of the next – then see yourself serving across the page as your stroke flows with perfect rhythm on the move.

STANCE •
Stability is enhanced by standing with your feet a good distance apart and your knees slightly flexed.

• PREPARATION
Push down into the court with your back foot, thus controlling the exact speed and direction of your weight transference.

SHAPE OF SHOT
The ball travels in a slight arc from behind the **baseline** into the service court diagonally opposite. After bouncing, the ball will probably reach the far baseline during its **second flight**.

SERVING AT TARGETS

AN EXERCISE
Position targets in 2 serving courts as shown. Serve 2 balls at each of the 3 targets and keep note of your score.

• POWER
Build power into your serve by initiating movement through the muscle groups in your legs and by following an upward use of your joints.

RHYTHM •
The continuous rhythm of the on-the-move serve creates momentum that can be used in serve and **volley** play.

SKILL 6

SERVICE RETURN

Definition: *Second only to the service in matchplay importance*

THE ABILITY TO CONSISTENTLY RETURN the serve is a practised art and has a great effect upon the outcome of every point. It is tactically vital to return every serve effectively but the serving strengths of your opponent govern the type and quality of your reply. You must, therefore, learn to adapt your basic **groundstrokes** to counteract the height, speed, spin, and placement of the serve. Initially, when returning serve, use your basic **forehand** and **backhand** drives and then adapt them to play the featured **returns**.

OBJECTIVE: To keep the ball in play and to take the initiative from the server. *Grips:* Basic Eastern forehand and backhand grips. *Rating* ••• to ••••

BLOCKED RETURN

Blocked returns are played with a short **take back** and volley-like punch. Stand just inside your **baseline** and take the ball early. **Block** through the back of the ball, aiming deep to the far baseline to nullify the server's advantage.

• CONTACT
Meet the ball early and out in front of your body.

RACKET CONTROL •
Keep your wrist firm and spread your first finger for extra control.

POSITION •
Step across with your front foot and **block** forwards.

BALL WATCH
Keep your eyes focused on the ball at impact.

• RACKET ANGLE
Racket face tilted back slightly to apply controlling underspin.

CHIPPED RETURN

The **chipped** return is very useful against high bouncing serves. Move inside your **baseline** and make a short, high **take back**, chipping down through the ball as it rises between waist and shoulder height.

FOOTWORK •
Feet can be parallel to or slightly across the line of flight of the ball.

ALTERNATIVE VIEW
This shows the importance of meeting the ball well in front of your body with your racket arm straight. Note the player's stability at impact, and how his racket stays with the ball after contact.

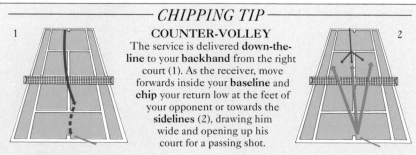

CHIPPING TIP

1

2

COUNTER-VOLLEY
The service is delivered **down-the-line** to your **backhand** from the right court (1). As the receiver, move forwards inside your **baseline** and **chip** your return low at the feet of your opponent or towards the **sidelines** (2), drawing him wide and opening up his court for a passing shot.

SKILL

6

TACTICAL LOB

SURPRISE RETURN
In 1, the ball is served to the backhand from the left court and the server runs forwards to volley, expecting the ball to be blocked, chipped or driven. A surprise topspin lobbed return (2) catches him flatfooted as he moves in. Return diagonally **cross court** or **down-the-line**.

LOBBED RETURN

Move forwards inside your **baseline** and form a short low **take back** before stepping in to sweep your racket head up the back of the ball, imparting heavy topspin.

IMPACT •
Take the high bouncing serve on the rise. This one is being met at about shoulder height.

STANCE •
Play your topspin lobbed return from a **sideways-on** position.

• **ANGLE**
Racket face almost vertical at impact, remains **open** in the high follow through.

• **GRIP**
Use your basic **Eastern backhand** grip for this shot, playing the return with a firm wrist. Here the shot is played firmly with a brushing action.

• **POSITION**
Step into the shot so that you can stay longer with the ball for extra control.

• CONTACT
Meet the ball with a
flattened out swing at
shoulder height.

BALANCE •
Let your spare hand help
to counter-balance your
hitting action.

DRIVEN RETURN

After returning serve with your basic
drives you will have no difficulty
adapting them to make the high and
low driven returns featured here. Try
them out on court, concentrating on
the actual hit and following the
technical pointers given.

• STANCE
Pivot **sideways-
on** and take
your racket back
quite high.

**HIGH
DRIVEN
RETURN**
The stance is
much straighter
than for the low
driven return.

LOW DRIVEN RETURN
To return a low bouncing serve to your
backhand, get down to ball level and step
positively into your shot. Meet the ball with
a slightly angled racket face to encourage lift.

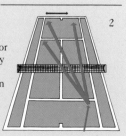

ATTACKING RETURN

TACTICS

1

2

After a short length serve (1), take the
ball early and hit it down the **sideline** or
cross court (2). The server is unlikely
to approach the net behind a poor-
length serve, so your attacking return
should put him on the defensive
and let you move up court. If he
serves even shorter, angle your
return to produce a winner.

SKILL

7

DAY 2

FOREHAND VOLLEY

Definition: *To play the ball during its* **first flight,** *before it has time to bounce*

THE VOLLEY SHOULD BE PLAYED like a boxer's jabbing punch. Advance towards the net and jab your racket head forwards to meet the ball before it bounces. Both **forehand** and **backhand volleys** are short, punched strokes that travel on a line from high to low, compared to the low to high swings of their equivalent **groundstrokes.**

OBJECTIVE: To hurry your opponent into making his next shot and, whenever possible, to place the ball beyond his reach from close quarters.
Rating ••

EYES •
Concentrate on
watching the ball as
you grab it with firm
control and accuracy.

COUNTERBALANCE •
Always use your spare hand to
balance your movements.

• HAND
Grab the ball to the
side and in front of
your body before it
falls towards the
ground.

GRAB THE BALL

The forehand **volley** action is just like catching the ball with your playing hand. Stand on opposite sides of the net to your partner, about 3m (10ft) back. Ask your partner to throw you a ball underarm at shoulder height. Reach forwards and grab it in front of you, as shown here.

• FEET
Step forwards and
across as you reach
out to grab the ball,
stabilizing the
movement with
your back foot.

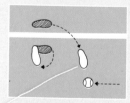

POSITIONING RACKET
Keep your **take back** short, getting your racket head behind the ball and slightly above your intended hitting height. Use the **forehand** grip and keep your wrist firm.

• POINTING
Released left hand points towards the oncoming ball.

Step 1

TAKE BACK

Pivot to your right until your racket is level with your shoulder. Release your left hand from the racket throat as you turn and keep your weight on your back foot.

• SUPPORT
Left foot steadying your turn but ready for step-in action.

BACK TO THE WALL
Put your partner against the wall and feed some balls to his forehand side. As he turns, the wall will restrict his take back. This set-up is a great way to cure "big swingers" on the volley.

FOOT WORK

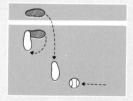

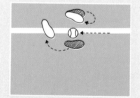

EASY BALL
To return an easy ball, turn on your right foot and step forwards with your left foot, parallel to the line of flight of the approaching ball.

WIDE BALL
Pivot to your right and step well across with your left foot when you realize the ball is some distance away. Rotate the upper body to maintain balance.

BODYLINE BALL
Turn on your left foot and then step back with your right to get **sideways-on** before leaning your weight forwards as you **volley** the ball.

SKILL
7

Step 2
THE HIT

Punch your racket head
forwards to meet the ball
in front of your body
between waist and
shoulder height.

CONTACT POINT •
Meet the ball
with the full
face of your
racket strings.

**THE GRAB-
PUNCH
POSITION**
Meet the ball
higher and closer
to your body
than you would
in **ground stroke** play. Try
to play the ball at eye level.

• RACKET ARM
Straighten your racket arm
at the hit. Punch down and
through the ball.

• BALANCE
Transfer your weight
positively over your
bent front knee.

• DIRECTION
Step in parallel or
slightly across the
ball's line of flight.

OFF THE WALL

CONTROL EXERCISES
Develop the accuracy and control of your forehand volley
by regularly practising against a wall. Stand 2m (6ft 6in)
away from the wall and practise the movements of
volleying – turning, stepping forwards and punching the
ball against the wall with your racket. Stay close to the wall
to limit your take back and improve racket-head control.

TARGET PRACTICE
When you can keep a 10- and then a 20-shot rally going,
try aiming for a target marked on the wall: this will further
develop your accuracy. Regular practice against a wall will
also strengthen your wrist.

TALKING TACTICS

A Sharply angled
crosscourt
B Deep crosscourt
C Down-the-line

VARIED APPROACHES

From a sound net position, volley deep down the **sideline** or across the court to pin your opponent in the **back court;** or try an angled **cross court** volley to place the ball beyond his reach.

SHAPE OF SHOT

In a volley the ball has only one flight; try to meet it above net height and aim your volley straight into your opponent's court.

— Step 3 —

FOLLOW THROUGH

The slight downward path of your racket adds underspin for shot control. Your follow through should be short.

• FOCUS
Head steady and eyes on the ball.

• PLAYING ARM
Keep your racket arm straight and the racket head above wrist level.

SHOULDER •
Hitting shoulder powers through.

FOREARM •
Use the forehand ("Shake hands") grip, with first finger spread and your elbow well away from the body. Go on to the **Continental** grip as your skill improves.

• LOWER BODY
Bend the knees for good stability and a low centre of gravity.

• BACK FOOT
Your back foot comes forwards when the stroke is complete to aid recovery.

• FRONT FOOT
Maintain a solid hitting platform in the follow through.

FOREHAND VOLLEY IN ACTION

Next to the smash, the **volley** is probably the most decisive shot in tennis and can be the match-winning shot in your repertoire. As soon as you have mastered the basic skills of volleying from the net position, you should start from further back and then practise running forwards to play your volleys on the move.

ANTICIPATION
Always carry your racket in front of you like a sword, ready for instant action.

• POSITIONING
Here the player is **split-stepping** in order to read the height and direction of his opponent's shot before he moves to intercept the ball.

• SELF CONTROL
Resist the temptation to take a swing at the ball when you are volleying on the move.

ALTERNATIVE VOLLEYS

LOW FOREHAND VOLLEY

To play a low **volley** even passably well you must crouch down, bending your knees, so that you can keep your wrist firm and your racket head level. Move into your low volley by stepping forwards and across with your front foot, angling your racket face slightly to apply some underspin as you punch through the back of the ball.

HIGH BACKHAND VOLLEY

In order to play a high volley really well, position yourself **sideways-on**, otherwise you may pull the ball down into the net or play it wide of the sidelines. High volleys need strong arms to punch the ball powerfully at shoulder height, so keep up your fitness training (see pp.16–19).

PACE
Control is vital so pace is imparted by playing forwards to the ball and not by the length of your **take back**.

SKILL

8

BACKHAND VOLLEY

Definition: *Like the forehand volley it is a short, punch-like stroke played mainly from the forecourt*

YOU MAY FIND that the **backhand volley** is easier to play than its counterpart on the **forehand** side, because when you take up the **sideways-on** position your playing arm leads the way and encourages positive action. As with all volleys, the major problem is time – you may have less than half a second to make your play. The natural crisp punch of the backhand volley makes it just the job for those quickfire volley **rallies** at the net where play is all reflex.

OBJECTIVE: To minimize the time for your opponent to play his next shot, and to win the point or force a defensive return. *Rating* ••

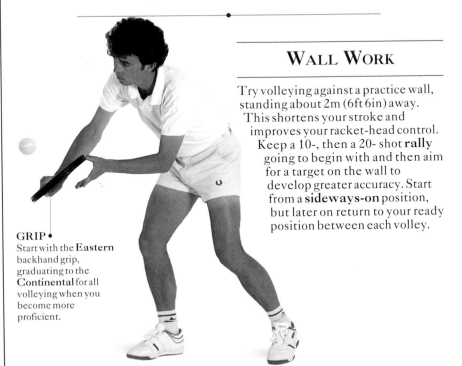

GRIP
Start with the **Eastern** backhand grip, graduating to the **Continental** for all volleying when you become more proficient.

WALL WORK

Try volleying against a practice wall, standing about 2m (6ft 6in) away. This shortens your stroke and improves your racket-head control. Keep a 10-, then a 20- shot **rally** going to begin with and then aim for a target on the wall to develop greater accuracy. Start from a **sideways-on** position, but later on return to your ready position between each volley.

SHADOWS AND SHOULDERS

EYE CHECK
In the take back with your eyes focused on the approaching ball, you should be able to see the outline of your racket head in the corner of your eye. Try this by shadowing your stroke. Stop when you complete your take back, and see if you can spot your racket head while still looking forward.

SHOULDER TURN
Avoid getting caught square-on at the net, and so dragging the ball down, by getting your hitting shoulder well round as you pivot **sideways-on** to the oncoming ball. Also keep your racket quite close to the body and your elbows flexed so that you can make an in-to-out punching action.

— Step 1 —

TAKE BACK

Turn **sideways-on** to the ball from your **ready position** and take your racket back level with your left shoulder while you support the racket at the throat with your non-playing hand.

• EYES
Look forwards at the ball.

WRIST •
Keep your wrist firm in the **backhand** grip.

• RACKET
Support the racket at the throat with your non-playing hand. Keep the racket head above hitting height.

KNEES •
Flex your knees slightly, with your back foot forming a firm base for hitting. For low balls bend your knees more.

• BALANCE
Keep your weight poised on the back leg ready for transfer on the hit.

FOOT •
Have your front foot ready to take the weight shift.

SKILL
8

Step 2
THE HIT

Releasing your left hand, step forwards and across slightly with your right foot, as you punch your racket head forwards to meet the ball, using the full face of your racket strings.

RACKET ARM•
Extend your playing arm, lock your wrist and keep your racket face steady.

• SUPPORT
Release your left hand to aid balance.

• PUNCHING ACTION
Prepare your racket head behind and slightly above the ball. Punch the racket head forwards and down through the back of the ball. Squeeze your grip, lock your wrist and keep your racket head up.

•WEIGHT SUPPORT
Transfer your weight fully over your bent front knee at the hit.

CONTACT
Meet the ball between waist and shoulder height.

• FOOTWORK
Try to keep parallel to, or slightly across, the line of the ball's flight.

FOCUS •
Eyes on
the ball.

NON-PLAYING ARM •
Left hand out for balance.

FOLLOW THROUGH

Let your racket head follow
through a short distance to
complete the **hitting
zone**, extending your
racket arm as you
play right through
the ball. The
slightly down-
ward action of
the racket with its bottom
edge leading will apply some
underspin to the ball for
added control.

POSTURE •
Lean your whole body
forwards as you play
through the ball.

STEP-IN •
A controlled step-
in helps you to
stay with the ball
in the follow
through.

STABILITY •
Keep your feet apart to aid
stability and lower your
centre of gravity.

TACTICAL VOLLEYING

ANGLED VOLLEYS
Volley the ball deep into the corners of your
opponent's court, especially from the mid-court
area. When you move in closer there will be
opportunities to play angled volleys. Aim to volley
straight most of the time, remembering that when
you do volley **cross court** you must be decisive as
it opens up a possible **down-the-line** passing shot
for your opponent, or even a wrong-footing crosscourt angle – if he can run down the ball.

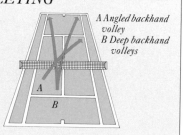

A Angled backhand
volley
B Deep backhand
volleys

BACKHAND VOLLEY IN ACTION

Backhands are usually seen as defensive strokes, but this is not the case once you have mastered playing the backhand **volley** in action. Develop the sequence in the same way as you worked on the **forehand volley**, starting from further back and then moving in quickly to volley. Here the player demonstrates the importance of getting well down to the ball and of transferring bodyweight into the shot. The slightly angled-back racket face at impact suggests that the player has played a first volley just inside the service line and will now move in closer to the net, looking for the kill with his second volley.

STEP-IN •
The **non-playing hand** is released and the racket head is punched down through the back of the ball.

CONCENTRATION •
Watching the ball is fundamental to the success of your on-the-move volleying skill, so keep your eyes on the ball all the way through the shot.

PREPARATION •
Always have your racket
ready to make your forward
play. On the high volley
take your racket back
higher than for the basic
volley to maintain the feel
of high-to-low action.

STANCE •
Stability is important, so
play the backhand volley
with your feet well apart and
body well balanced.

LOW BACKHAND VOLLEY

THE STROKE
It is more difficult to attack a low ball than
one above the net but you do not have to
play defensively. Bend your knees, getting
your eyes down to ball level, then step in
and punch your racket head under and
through the ball. Lead with the bottom
edge of the racket to apply underspin and
create lift for net clearance. Success
depends on a firm wrist and a controlled
racket head, held at or above wrist level.

SKILL

9 LOB DEFENCE

Definition: *Groundstroke that sends the ball high in the air. Predominantly a defensive shot*

THE LOB IS NOT SIMPLY a last line of defence for tossing the ball high in the air and praying for a miracle. Use your lobs like paratroopers, drop them behind your opponent's front line of attack and close in on the net yourself as he scampers back to base on the defence. Don't wait until he's camping out in the **forecourt** either – an early lob can play havoc with his confidence. The lob is a fuller stroke than the drive, with a lower **take back** and a higher finish.

OBJECTIVE: Impenetrable defence and surprise counter-attack. Grip: as for the forehand and backhand drives. *Rating* •••

Step 2

TAKE BACK

Begin your stroke like a drive, taking your racket back as you turn **sideways-on**. Relax the elbow of your playing arm at the end of the **take back**, letting your racket form a low **loop**. Step in and start to swing the racket head forwards in a steep upwards path.

GRIP •
Use the **Eastern** ("Shake hands") grip, and keep the racket face open.

GET LOW •
Get down and **loop** low.

STANCE •
Step in on to your flexed front knee as you begin the forward swing from the take back.

UPPER BODY
Keep your head steady and your eyes on the ball. Left hand comes back but still acts as a stabilizer as you turn into the hit.

Step 3
THE HIT

Leading with the bottom edge of your racket face, let the racket swing forwards in a steep upwards path, to meet the ball in front of your leading hip. Squeeze your grip at impact to steady your wrist. Time your swing to meet the ball between knee and waist height as it falls.

• PLATFORM
Your left foot provides a sound hitting platform, aiding the height and depth of your lob.

• RACKET ANGLE
Keep the racket face angled back for lift – but not too much or the lob will fall short.

• STANCE
Get down and really sit into the shot.

• HAND BALANCE
Point the left hand towards the ball to help keep your balance.

FLIGHT PATH

7m (20 ft)

The basic lob carries a little topspin by virtue of the steep low to high swing and the racket face angle. It should travel in an even arc, clearing the net by about 7m (20ft), and land just inside the opposite **baseline.** You should get a fairly high **second flight** after the bounce.

HIGH FOLLOW THROUGH
The drive-like beginning of the lob can often catch your opponent off guard, but the follow through is a dead giveaway. After impact, let your racket swing up through the **hitting zone**, as you straighten your legs and really stay with the ball, sending it high in the air. Finish the stroke with racket above head.

BACKHAND LOB IN ACTION

Perform a basic **backhand lob** by simply adapting the backhand drive and producing a similar stroke to the **forehand lob**. Switch to your backhand grip, using your spare hand during the **take back**. Here the player has moved wide from a central base to play an advanced defensive lob with underspin, to counter an opponent's net attack. The player's speed to the ball combined with his racket control at impact have produced a perfectly measured lob that can easily turn defence into attack.

LOBBING TACTICS

TWO STYLES

Generally, **lob** deep as short lobs are snapped up by net players. Lob over your opponent's non-playing shoulder to his backhand corner because the smash is more difficult to play if you have to move diagonally backwards to reach the ball. Here an attacking backhand lob is played diagonally (*A*) and a deeper forehand lob is played **down-the-line** (*B*). The backhand lob can be played with topspin to make the ball bounce sharply away from your opponent.

CONCENTRATE •
Keep your eyes on the ball throughout the **hitting zone** and watch to see the effect of your **lob**.

FOLLOW THROUGH •
Beautifully balanced in the **follow through**, the player has complete control of his movement, his racket and the ball. The basic backhand grip has been used to play this advanced on-the-move backhand lob.

MOBILIZE
Having tracked the ball's flight and mentally marked your opponent's point of aim, move off quickly in a diagonally forward run to intercept the ball shortly after the bounce.

RACKET ANGLE
Having decided to play the ball early with underspin, prepare your racket with a short high take back as you approach the **hitting area**.

HITTING PLATFORM
Get right down to make the shot, with your legs wide apart and a low centre of gravity. With the racket face angled back, underspin is then applied.

SKILL

10 SMASH ATTACK

DAY 2

Definition: *The aggressive antidote to the lob*

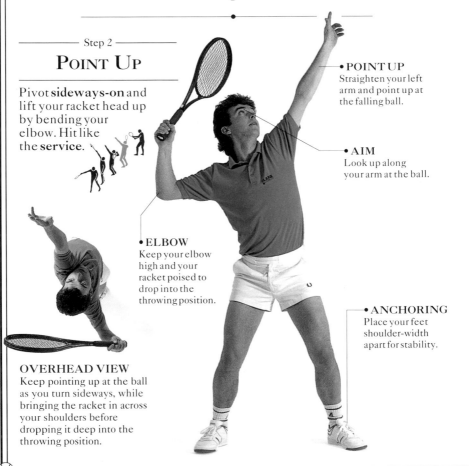

THE OVERHEAD SMASH is a roving assassin waiting to pounce on, and eliminate, any weak lobs put up by an opponent who is under siege from your net attack. When he uses defensive or offensive lobs in an attempt to break out of his predicament, you must smash deep using an overarm action similar to the serve.

OBJECTIVE: To maintain an attacking initiative and to win points outright.
Rating ••••

―――――― Step 2 ――――――
POINT UP

Pivot **sideways-on** and lift your racket head up by bending your elbow. Hit like the **service**.

• **POINT UP**
Straighten your left arm and point up at the falling ball.

• **AIM**
Look up along your arm at the ball.

• **ELBOW**
Keep your elbow high and your racket poised to drop into the throwing position.

• **ANCHORING**
Place your feet shoulder-width apart for stability.

OVERHEAD VIEW
Keep pointing up at the ball as you turn sideways, while bringing the racket in across your shoulders before dropping it deep into the throwing position.

FANCY FOOTWORK

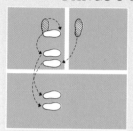 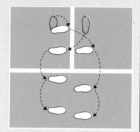

SIDE STEP
To line up smashes quickly you need to keep **sideways-on** to the ball as you position yourself behind and below the ball. Footwork for the side skip, or side step, is simple. Just turn and move with a side-together-side foot action.

CROSS OVER
Footwork for the cross over needs practice but it really keeps you sideways-on. After turning, cross your left foot in front of your right. Side-step with your right. Repeat until you are in position.

CONTACT POINT •
Hit the ball ahead of you at racket arm's reach.

GRIP •
Start with the modified **Eastern** grip and progress in time to the serving grip.

• NATURAL INCLINE
Stretch and incline your whole body.

Step 4

THE HIT

Fully extend your racket arm as you throw your racket head up to meet the ball, with the full face of the racket strings. Hit the ball out in front of you and finish the stroke like a **service**.

• SHOULDER IT
Let your playing shoulder turn powerfully in to the hit.

• BALANCE
Weight forwards and legs straight.

SHAPE OF SHOT

B   *A*

A Net smash B Deep smash

From close in on the net you can angle your smash or make it bounce over your opponent's head. From further back, smash the ball deep and try to maintain your attack.

• STABILIZER
Your back foot stabilizes the basic smash at impact.

• TIPTOES
Get up on your tiptoes at impact.

JUMP SMASH IN ACTION

The jump smash epitomizes on-the-move action, yet below, the player is very still in mid-air as he smashes the ball. This type of smash is ideal for overcoming any lack of reach you might have and for dealing effectively with deep **lobs** that might otherwise have left you stranded in the **forecourt**. In order to play the shot really well, you must develop speed and agility to move backwards in a **sideways-on** position and power in your legs for leaping high in the air. On court, turn sideways-on as soon as the lob goes up and use the **split step** for your run-back.

• FOLLOW THROUGH
After hitting up and over the ball, land on your left foot and follow through in similar fashion to your basic smash.

LEG ACTION •
Let your right leg swing past your left in a scissor-like action when you throw your racket head up to meet the ball above and in front of you at full racket-arm's reach.

SMASHING TACTICS

LETHAL WEAPON

The smash can only be used against **lobs** or high bouncing balls, so develop an attacking game that forces opponents to put up defensive lobs. Aim for your opponent's **backhand** corner – if he begins to anticipate this, turn your wrist more and slice your smash to his **forehand** corner. High lobs should be smashed after the bounce, but use a jump smash with balls you would not otherwise be able to retrieve. If inside the **service line**, try angling your smashes towards the **sidelines**.

FLIGHT POSITION

As you become airborne, let your racket head drop into the full throwing position and keep your left arm out for balance.

TIMING

With your racket head prepared, jump off the back leg to smash the ball before it can dip behind you.

SKILL

11

DAY 2

APPROACH PLAY

Definition: *A modified groundstroke for net attack*

IN APPROACH PLAY the placement of your shot is crucial to the success of any attack. Allow your position and the height at which you play the ball to dictate the stroke, but shorten the **take back** for extra control. Having reached the **forecourt** use the **volleying** skills that you have already mastered.

OBJECTIVE : To set up opportunities for decisive volleying.
Rating • • • • *Grips:* As for groundstrokes

——— Steps 1-2 ———

APPROACH SHOT

The shot depicted here is a backhand slice. Play a short firm swing from the shoulder, slightly down, through the back of the ball.

THE HIT •
Meet the ball in front of you with your wrists locked and your racket face tilted back.

• FOOTWORK
Having prepared on your back foot, step crisply forwards and slightly across with your front foot as you make the shot.

• RACKET
Let the racket head rise as you finish the stroke.

Steps 3-5

FOLLOW THROUGH

You should be totally committed to a net advance when an **approach shot** beckons, so follow quickly in the direction of your shot as the stroke finishes. Your back foot follows through as part of a continuous move towards a sound position.

— AREAS OF PLAY —

Advisable

Possible

Inadvisable

APPROACH TACTICS
The basic rule is never to approach the net from a deep position. Aim to get where you want to be before your opponent strikes the ball; if this is not possible, then split-step early.

SPLIT-STEP •
Follow the line of your **approach shot** in, but **split-step** (see p.82) as your opponent makes his play. Be still, attentive, and on balance as the ball is struck.

• WRIST
Keep your wrist steady in the **hitting zone** and in the short **follow through**.

BALANCE •
To **volley** successfully behind approach play get your weight forwards into the hit and keep your body steady at impact.

IMPACT •
Aim to attack the ball at the highest point possible.

SKILL

12 SERVE & VOLLEY

DAY 2

Definition: *A two-pronged attack to end points swiftly*

THE SERVE AND VOLLEY is a decisive tactic that can give you control of the net area. As with **approach shots**, it is accuracy, pace and depth of service that dictate subsequent volleying success. Give yourself time to reach a good position; serve at three quarter speed to your opponent's weaker stroke, applying slice for extra control.

OBJECTIVE: To put pressure on your opponent.
Rating ••••• *Grips:* Serve and groundstroke

--------- Step 1 ---------
TAKE BACK

Take up your serving stance, selecting your service type and direction. Pin-point your forward run and try to reach a destinaton inside your **service line** before the ball is returned.

•PLACE UP
Place the ball up further forwards to develop more impetus, but do not overreach or hurry your serving action.

--------- Step 2 ---------
FOLLOW THROUGH

As your back foot swings across the **baseline** when you serve, it becomes the first step of your forward run. Cross your service line in about six steps and be ready to play a **volley** that will keep you on the offensive.

SPLIT-STEPPING OPTIONS

TECHNIQUE
Split stepping is simply interrupting your forward run by planting your feet shoulder-width apart to regain a basic ready position. Split step early in order to be perfectly balanced for instant lateral movement.

The illustration above shows that the player can move to his right, to cut off a **cross court** return, or to his left, to backhand volley an attempted passing shot **down-the-line**. Here the volleys are played from a deep position.

Step 4

THE HIT

If playing from a deep position, aim to volley towards a corner, keeping your opponent back while you approach the net. Punish short high returns with aggressive volleys.

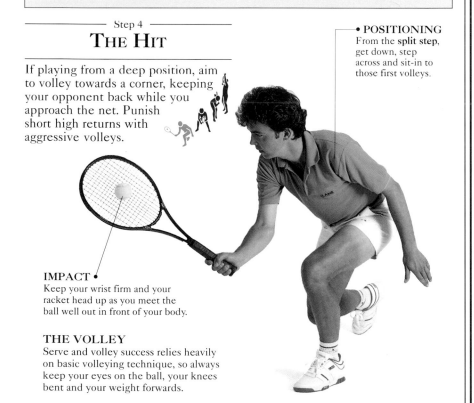

• POSITIONING
From the **split step**, get down, step across and sit-in to those first volleys.

IMPACT •
Keep your wrist firm and your racket head up as you meet the ball well out in front of your body.

THE VOLLEY
Serve and volley success relies heavily on basic volleying technique, so always keep your eyes on the ball, your knees bent and your weight forwards.

AFTER THE WEEKEND

*Now you have had some practical experience of tennis,
here are some rules and basic playing procedures*

NOW YOU HAVE COMPLETED THE COURSE, try the games and
advanced strokes described on the following pages. If you are keen
to progress further, join a tennis club. This is an ideal way to
develop your game and mix with others who have similar interests.

RULES OF THE GAME

SCORING

The first point is 15, the second 30, the
third 40 and the fourth point won makes it
game. The server's score is called first, i.e.
if the server wins the first point, the score
is 15-"love" (15-0), except in a tie-break
when the player ahead is named first. If
each player has 3 points (40-40), "deuce"
is called and one player must gain 2 points
in a row to win. The first is an "advantage"
point, but if the next point is lost, the score
returns to deuce. A set is decided when
one player wins 6 games with a margin of
at least 2 games.

If the score reaches 5–5, then play
continues until one player is 2 games
ahead. Matches are normally the best of
3 sets, but can be the best of 5.

TIE-BREAK

Tie-breaks are used when the score in a
set reaches 6–6. Scoring is numerical and
the first player to win 7 points, with a 2
point margin, wins the game. The player
who serves first in the tie-break serves for 1
point only and service then alternates each
2 points. Change ends after every 6 points.

Always use the correct playing procedure. Toss a coin or spin a racket to decide who serves first. The winner of the toss can choose to serve, receive, take an end or can ask his opponent to choose. If you choose to serve, your opponent decides which end of the court to receive from for the first game. Serve from behind your **baseline**, starting in the right court for the first point, the **left court** for the second and so on. The service ball must be struck before it bounces and must go over the net and land in the **service** court diagonally opposite. If you serve a fault, you can serve again but a **double fault** gives your opponent the point. A receiver can stand anywhere in his court but cannot **volley** the serve or let it bounce twice. Alternate serving and receiving throughout the match and change ends after every odd-numbered game.

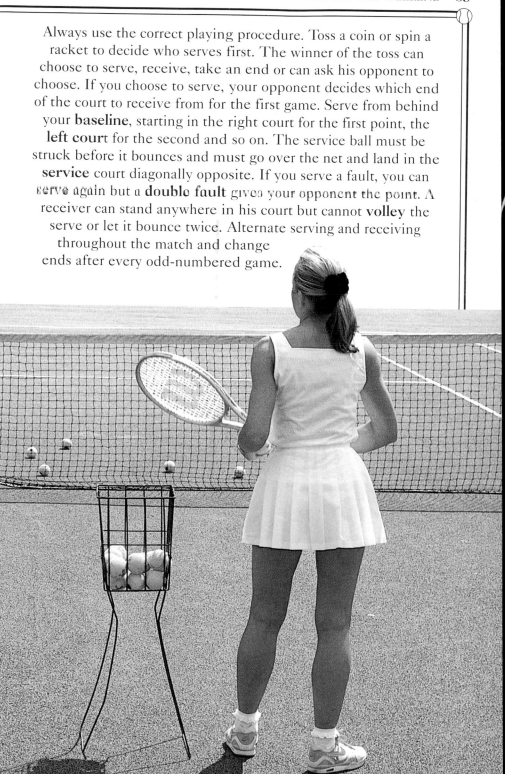

PLAYING THE GAME

Tennis is a game where tactics and positioning are vital if you are to be successful. You've learned the strokes, now play the game!

PRACTICE IS IMPORTANT, but the object of any course of instruction is to get you playing the game as soon as possible. Over your weekend you have learnt to play many different strokes, but it is only when you actually play matches against an opponent that you can determine your strengths and weaknesses. Your natural abilities will dictate how you initially approach matchplay and you may find that you prefer to play either a **baseline** or a **volleying** game. Tactically, tennis is a game of control and the player making the fewest mistakes is likely to win. While striving to make as few mistakes as possible is a sound approach, it can lead to a purely defensive game. Attacking play produces winning shots that unsettle the rhythm of the defensive-minded opponent, so try to combine the two styles mixing defence with attack as the game dictates.

ON THE COURT

Tactically, the area behind and up to your **baseline** is the **backcourt**, the area between your service line and the net is the **forecourt**, and the area in between is **no man's land**.

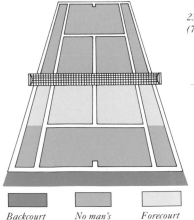

23.77m (78ft)

8.23m (27ft)

91cm (3ft)

6.4m (21ft)

5.48m (18ft)

1.37m (4ft 6in)

10.97m (36ft)

Backcourt   *No man's land*   *Forecourt*

NO MAN'S LAND
If you have to play a shot in **no man's land**, play it and get out fast or you may be caught with the ball at your feet and no time to play your next shot.

COURT AREA
The doubles court is the same length as the singles, but 2.74m (9ft) wider. The service courts are the same size for both games, but use the **alley** in doubles when rallying.

CENTREPOINT TACTIC

Play the shot, then move to the **centrepoint** – midway between the 2 extremes of your opponent's return. Use a good tactical shot to ensure your next centrepoint is close. The volleyer below has found a good centrepoint.

— WRONG FOOTING —

TACTICAL OPTION.

The receiver (below) has returned the ball **down-the-line** and a bit short, so opening up the possibility of a wide-angled **crosscourt** response. As he runs to take up a central position well beyond his **centre mark**, his opponent plays the ball down-the-line for a wrong-footing winner.

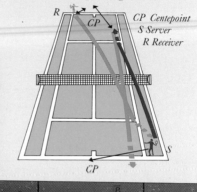

CP Centepoint
S Server
R Receiver

CENTREPOINT AWARENESS

DON'T GET CAUGHT OUT!

A danger with the **centrepoint** tactic is being caught out on the way to your next centrepoint. This need not happen if you are still and attentive whenever your opponent is playing the ball. Here, the server plays a wide service to the right-handed receiver who replies with a deep **crosscourt** forehand return so that his next centrepoint is quite close. If the receiver had chosen to play **down-the-line**, the position midway between the possible replies would be been a metre or so beyond the **centre mark**.

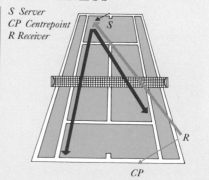

S Server
CP Centepoint
R Receiver

PLAYING DOUBLES

A team game between two pairs of tennis players where strategy and tactics are of the utmost importance

IN CONTRAST TO THE SINGLES GAME, doubles is about team work, and you must work together. Try to play level with your partner, aiming to get to the net quickly and to remain there until you have won the point. If you are in doubt about placing a shot during the **rally**, aim between your opponents, so creating possible confusion about which one of them should play the ball. A successful doubles team places far more emphasis on team work and tactics than on the sheer physical strength that is associated with the singles game.

SERVING POSITIONS

One person plays in the right court, the other in the left. Each player is responsible for the shots in his half. If you cross to your partner's half, then he should move to your court to cover shots to that area.

SERVER
Assume the service stance halfway between the **centre mark** (see p.14) and your nearest doubles **sideline**. This position will give you the best opportunity of covering all of the returns to your half of the court.

SERVER'S PARTNER
Take up an attack position in the other half of the court 2.7m (9ft) from the net and halfway between the centre line and your nearest doubles **sideline**. From here you can play aggressive **volleys** and smashes.

RECEIVING POSITIONS

When receiving, start from the **baseline** area, while your partner can take up a mid-court position. Having decided who receives in which court keep these positions for the set.

RECEIVER'S PARTNER

Stand just inside the service line, halfway between the centre line and the doubles **sideline**. From here you can advance to the net or retreat behind the **baseline**. You can also counter-**volley** if the server's partner intercepts your partner's return.

RECEIVER

To return first services your receiving position should be the same as for singles play but when returning second services move forwards inside your **baseline** to take up a more attacking position.

TACTICAL FORMATION

Left-hand court serve

PLAYING THE DOUBLES GAME

When serving, try to get a high percentage of your first serves into court. Sacrifice speed if necessary, but depth and accuracy are vital. When receiving, keep your returns low over the net, unless you are playing a lob, and aim 80 per cent of them **cross court** away from the server's partner. If following in behind your serve or return is difficult try playing a **groundstroke** or two before advancing.

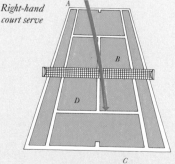

Right-hand court serve

COURT POSITIONS

These two diagrams illustrate the 4 basic positions for the attacking and receiving teams before the start of a point.

A = Server
B = Server's partner
C = Receiver
D = Receiver's partner

ADVANCED STROKES

Technically more difficult strokes that demand a
higher level of skill in matchplay situations

ONCE YOU HAVE MASTERED THE BASIC TECHNIQUES of strokeplay, you
will be keen to have a go at the more advanced strokes in order to
further develop your playing skills. If you have started a fitness
training programme, established the habit of daily stretching and
joined a tennis club for regular practice sessions, these will not be
such difficult skills to master. An advanced stroke is one that, when
compared to the more basic strokes, has a greater degree of
difficulty in either matchplay performance, or technical execution,
or both. However, if you have methodically worked your way
through the weekend course you will be well equipped to tackle
these three advanced **groundstrokes**. You may have a flair for one
of them and will be able to use it in your matches. There are many
other advanced strokes that you can use in singles and doubles play,
including the topspin serve and the backhand smash. With practice,
plus advice from a coach, you should soon be able to master them.

FOREHAND HALF-VOLLEY

The **take back** must be short and low,
with your racket head at wrist level. Let
your knees bend as you turn on your
rear foot and get down low to meet the
ball just after the
bounce, keeping
your wrist firm.

• STANCE
Crouch down, with your
left hand out for balance.

GRIP •
Get your wrist and
racket head in line.

• FOOTWORK
Front foot forward,
and back knee low.

BACKHAND DROP SHOT

The angle of your racket face is crucial. Tilt it back and push the racket head downwards under the ball. This adds underspin to the ball, which is deflected up and off the racket strings and drops just over the net with very little bounce. Follow through for a short distance.

• EYES
Watch the ball with even more concentration when playing advanced strokes

BALANCE •
Release the **non-playing hand** for balance.

WEIGHT •
Transfer your body weight into the shot over bent front knee.

• CONTACT
Meet the ball at waist height and have your racket face open.

TAKE BACK
Take your racket back about head high, with your racket face angled back to apply underspin.

• STABILITY
Keep your back toe in contact with the court to provide stability.

TOPSPIN BACKHAND DRIVE

TECHNIQUE
This is an attacking stroke which requires perfect timing. The ball is played in an outwards and upwards brushing action to produce the topspin effect. Use your full **backhand** grip and take your racket back below your intended hitting height.

THE HIT
Step in parallel to the ball's flight and, with your weight well forwards over your front knee, swing your racket head steeply up through the back of the ball with the racket face almost vertical. As the racket swings on, let your wrist roll the face over slightly. Racket face angle is crucial – if it is too open, underspin, instead of topspin, will be applied.

GLOSSARY

A

• **Alley** The area of the court between the singles and doubles sidelines, also known as the "tramlines".
• **Approach shot** A groundstroke played just before you approach the net to volley.

B

• **Backcourt** Incorporates no man's land but is tactically the area behind the baseline from which the baseliner plays.
• **Backhand** For right-handed players this is a stroke played on the left hand side of the body, with the back of the hand towards the net.
• **Baseline** The line at each end of the court that runs parallel to the net and marks the boundaries lengthwise of the playing area.
• **Block** Short punched groundstroke used to return a fast travelling ball.

C

• **Centre mark** A 10.16cm (4in) line that marks the centre of the baseline.
• **Centrepoint** A mid-point between two angles of a possible shot.
• **Chip** A short underspun ground stroke usually played to return a spinning serve or high bouncing ball.
• **Closed** Applies to racket face angle.
• **Continental** Name of the service grip that originated in Britain.
• **Cross court** A stroke played across the court from right court to right court or left court to left court.

D

• **Double-fault** Two successive service faults from the same court.
• **Double-handed** A player who keeps both hands on the racket handle during the forward swing of the racket.
• **Down-the-line** Shot played approximately parallel to the sidelines as opposed to cross-court.
• **Drop shot** A shot played short, dropping into the forecourt – which bounces close to the net.

E

• **Eastern** A basic tennis grip originating on the East coast of the USA.

F

• **First flight** The initial flight of the ball after it has been struck by the racket.
• **Follow through** refers to the continuing travel of the racket after the ball has been struck .
• **Foot fault** A fault called when a player steps on to or over the baseline while serving, before actually striking the ball.
• **Forecourt** The area of the court between the net and the service lines.
• **Forehand** A stroke played on the right hand side of the body for right handed players and on the left hand side for left handed players.

G

• **Groundstroke** A forehand or backhand stroke played after the ball has bounced.

H

• **Half-volley** A groundstroke played immediately after the ball has bounced.
• **Hitting area/zone** The general area of the court where you strike the ball.
• **Hopper** The container for balls in a ball machine or a separate basket for holding large quantities of tennis balls.

L

• **Left court** The area to the left of the centre line from the net to the baseline.
• **Let** When play is interrupted a let is called and the point replayed. When a service let is called, only the service in question is replayed.
• **Lob** A ball sent high in the air.
• **Loop** In groundstroke play the racket forms a loop as backswing and forward swing are joined in one continuous movement.
• **Love** In tennis scoring love means nothing, hence love–thirty is 0–30.

N

•**No man's land** The area between the service line and the baseline.
•**Non-playing hand** The player's supporting hand – vital for balance.

O

•**Open** Refers to racket face angle when a greater hitting area is presented to the ball.

P

•**Palming the ball** Hitting or playing the ball with the palm of your hand.
•**Place-up** The ball toss during the service.

R

•**Rally** An exchange of strokes after the service has been delivered.
•**Ready position** A position of readiness adopted to receive the service, which acts as a starting point for all groundstrokes and volleys.
•**Return** Primarily the stroke that returns the serve but can be used to describe any shot during a rally.
•**Run the ball down** To chase a ball that is some distance away.

S

•**Second flight** The flight of the ball after it has bounced.
•**Service** The stroke used at the start of each point.
•**Service line** A service boundary line.
•**Set** There are six games in a set and three or five sets in a match.
•**Shadowing** Going through the motions without hitting the ball, hence "shadowing the stroke".
•**"Shake hands"** Refers to the basic Eastern Forehand Drive grip.
•**Sidelines** The boundary lines of the court lengthwise.
•**Sidespin** When one side of the ball rotates against the air resistance, it is forced to swerve to the opposite side; e.g. a ball approaching with left hand spin will swerve from right to left.
•**Sideways-on** Applies to being parallel to the approaching ball's flight.
•**Spin** The way that a ball rotates.
•**Split step** Assuming the ready position before changing the direction of a run.

•**Stay with the ball** Refers to following through in the direction of your shot after hitting the ball.
•**Sweet-spot** The central position on the racket face for producing the perfect shot.
•**Swinging** The forward action of a basic groundstroke.

T

•**Take back** The preparation of the stroke prior to the forward swing.
•**Take-up** The preparation of the racket in serving and smashing prior to the racket head being lowered into the "throwing" position.
•**The "T"** The central area where the centre line joins the service line.
•**The "V"** The angle made between the thumb and first finger of the hand.
•**Tie-break** This is a point scoring system designed to shorten the length of a set. It is usually brought into operation when the set score reaches six games all.

V

•**Volley** To volley the ball is to hit it before it bounces.

W

•**Western** An American type of grip that finds the palm of the hand more underneath the handle than behind it.
•**Wide-body** These are rackets that have a very broad side-on dimension .
•**Wrong-foot** This is to send an opponent the wrong way.

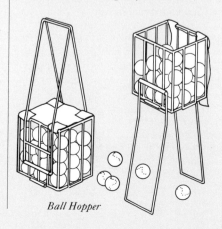

Ball Hopper

INDEX

GETTING IN TOUCH

The Professional Tennis
Coaches' Association
of Great Britain
21 Glencairn Court
Lansdown Road
Cheltenham, Glou.GL50 2NB

The Lawn Tennis
Association Trust
The Queen's Club
West Kensington
London W14 9EG

Dunlop Slazenger Int.
Challenge Court
Business Park 9
Barnett Wood Lane
Leatherhead
Surrey KT22 7LW

ACKNOWLEDGMENTS

Paul Douglas and Dorling Kindersley would like to thank the following for
their help and support in the preparation and production of this book.

Alan Douglas for modelling the action sequences and advanced strokes.
Ross McCue for modelling basic techniques and fitness exercises.
Ferida Loh for modelling stretching exercises and double-handed shots.
Chris Lane Tennis and Health Club, Surrey, for location facilities.
Dunlop Slazenger International Ltd., Dunlop Footwear Ltd., Prince (UK)
Ltd., Nike (UK) Ltd., Pro-Kennex (UK) Ltd., for use of equipment.
Larry Fulcher School of Tennis, Ipswich, Suffolk, for use of ball machine.

Plough Studios, Clapham, London SW4 for indoor photography facilities.
London Workshops for the high speed flash.
Rob Shone, Craig Austin, Paul Dewhurst, Pete Sargent for line drawings.
Phil Hunt and Damien Moore for editorial assistance.